Broadcasting and the Media

The Insider Career Guides is a dynamic series of books designed to give you the inside track on individual careers – how to get in, how to get on, even how to get out.

Based on the real-life experiences of people actually working in these fields, each title offers a combination of hard practical information and insider information on working culture, the pros and cons of different areas of work, prospects for promotion, etc.

Other titles in the series:

Advertising, Marketing and PR
Karen Holmes

Banking and the City
Karen Holmes

The Environment
Melanie Allen

Information and Communications Technology
Jacquetta Megarry

Retailing
Liz Edwards

Sport
Robin Hardwick

Travel and Tourism
Karen France

About the Series Editor
Following a successful career as a teacher and lecturer in the UK and the Far East, Karen Holmes now works as a freelance writer, editor and project manager. Specialising in learning and careers, she has authored a range of careers literature for publishers and other commercial organisations.

Broadcasting and the Media

by

Paul Redstone

PARK LEARNING CENTRE
UNIVERSITY OF GLOUCESTERSHIRE
PO Box 220, The Park
Cheltenham GL50 2RH
Tel: 01242 714333

First published in 2000 by
The Industrial Society
Robert Hyde House
48 Bryanston Square
London WIH 7LN

© The Industrial Society 2000

ISBN I 85835 867 I

British Library Cataloguing-in-Publication Data.
A catalogue record for this book is available from the
British Library.

Typeset by: The Midlands Book Typesetting Company
Printed by: Cromwell Press
Cover by: Sign Design
Cover image by: Photonica

The Industrial Society is a Registered Charity No. 290003

CONTENTS

INTRODUCTION

Communication is vitally important. Better communications have made it possible for businesses to become global in scope and reach out to new markets. The way we do business has changed forever. In this worldwide marketplace, information and communication have become all-important, and the role of the media is a central one.

Of course, it is not just the world of business that has been affected. The media are increasingly important elements in our lives. Their influence is everywhere. The media are our eyes on the world – it is largely through them that we build up a picture of the world around us. They can educate us, inform us and lead us to explore new horizons.

The media industries are dynamic and exciting environments in which to work. New developments are changing the direction of the industries and opening up new realms of opportunity. Things are moving fast and the last few years have seen unprecedented change in the way we communicate. The possibilities are limited only by the scope of our imagination.

This book is for anyone interested in a career in broadcasting and other media. Whether you are considering a career change, leaving school, about to graduate or simply curious, you will find plenty of useful information and advice to help you every step of the way.

The book is divided into three sections: *The Job, The Person* and *Getting in, Getting on... Getting out.* At the end you will find useful contact addresses and websites, and a *Jargon buster* to help decipher some of the technical terms you may encounter in the industry. Above all, this is a practical book. There are useful tips and checklists, and revealing case studies of industry professionals to give you the inside story.

Part One, *The Job,* gives an overview of the industries and their employment possibilities, including:

- the history and future of the media
- major media employers
- job descriptions and salaries
- new media.

Part Two, *The Person,* looks at the skills media employers want and the people employed in the industry. It examines:

- skill requirements
- how to assess your skills
- how to decide if working in the media is for you
- the low-down on freelancing.

Part Three, *Getting in, Getting on… Getting out,* takes a look at:

- education and training
- finding and applying for vacancies
- interview success
- moving up the career ladder
- options for leaving the industry.

part one the job

the job

'One machine can do the work of 50 ordinary men. No machine can do the work of one extraordinary man.'

Elbert Hubbard (1856–1915), US writer and printer

Introduction

The title of this book is *The Insider Career Guide to Broadcasting and the Media*. Before going any further, let's examine what the terms mean.

Media are channels through which information is transmitted to the public. This blanket term incorporates many different forms of communication. Broadcasting naturally comes under this heading, but for practical purposes it is useful to make a distinction between it and the other forms of media we are looking at.

This book focuses on three key areas:

- radio and TV broadcasting
- printed media
- electronic media.

There are areas this book does not cover, perhaps most notably the film industry. However, even if you do want to pursue a career in film, you will still find much information and guidance in this book that is relevant and helpful. Think of this book as a useful starting point for planning your media career strategy.

In Part One, we take an overview of the industries and look at some specific aspects of work within them.

A BRIEF HISTORY OF THE MEDIA

Radio

Broadcasting has its origins back in the 19th century. In the 1880s and 1890s, the Telefon-Hirmondo cable system broadcast entertainment programmes via the telephone system. A similar system was later introduced in the US.

The existence of radio waves was predicted by James Clerk Maxwell as early as 1865, his theories only being proved correct some 20 years later by Heinrich Hertz. Much of the early ground-breaking work on radio transmission was done by Guglielmo Marconi, although he had not actually transmitted anything other than the dots and dashes of the Morse system. The first true broadcast was achieved by Reginald Fessenden on Christmas Eve 1906, and featured Fessenden reading poetry and playing the violin.

It was not until around 1919 that radio really got underway, with stations broadcasting in Europe and America. In 1922, a key year, the French began broadcasting from the Eiffel Tower, there were transmissions from Moscow and the BBC was formed, transmitting the world's first truly national radio programme. The BBC was Britain's sole legal broadcaster until the Sound Broadcasting Act of 1972, which cleared the way for independent local radio stations.

Television

The first experiments in television broadcasting were carried out by Scotsman John Logie Baird. He broadcast the first ever TV picture, a 30-line mechanically scanned image, in 1924. Research was well underway in America at around the same time, with Vladimir Zworykin pioneering the development of an all-electronic system.

The BBC began regular broadcasting in 1936, but stopped at the start of the Second World War. Programming was resumed in 1946. TV remained a minority medium in this country until 1953, when a huge number of people bought TV sets specifically to see the Coronation. TV was firmly entrenched in British culture from then on.

Lord Reith was the BBC's first, and probably most influential, director general. Through him, the concept of public service broadcasting became ingrained in the organisation. Under Reith, the BBC began its mission 'to inform, educate and entertain'. This maxim remains the BBC's guiding principle to this day.

The BBC had the monopoly on TV broadcasting until 1955, when the new Tory Government's Television Bill allowed the formation of regional independent commercial television companies. ITV's more populist programming was an instant success. The duopoly of the BBC and ITV continued until the launch of Channel 4 in 1982. Channel 5 was eventually launched in 1996.

One of the most significant recent developments was the 1990 Broadcasting Act, brought in by Margaret Thatcher's Conservative Government. This forced the selling off of the ITV companies to the highest bidder. It also brought in the rule that TV companies must buy at least 25% of their programming from independent producers. The Act was the foundation for increasing deregulation and the introduction of cable and satellite TV into this country.

Newspapers and periodicals

The history of printed media is a long one – the very earliest newspaper is thought to have been the hand-written *Acta Diurna* ('daily acts'), which appeared in ancient Rome around 59BC. The development of the printing press by the German Johann Gutenberg in the mid-15th century paved the way for mass printing and the emergence of the newspaper as we know it today. Germany was the European newspaper pioneer, printing papers from the late 15th century. British newspapers began around 1620. Their development was stifled by the Civil War and Cromwell's subsequent suppression of all but parliament-licensed periodicals. In 1695, parliament decided not to renew the Licensing Act, opening the floodgates for a free press.

Some important developments occurred in America in the 19th century. The 1830s saw the start of the 'Penny Press', which gave the public human interest and sensationalist stories for a very low price. The tabloids were born. 'New Journalism', epitomised by Joseph Pulitzer and William Randolph Hearst, began in America after the Civil War. This style was opinion-led, with an emphasis on interviews and gossip columns, and gave a powerful voice to the editor. New journalism was introduced to Britain in 1880, when W. T. Stead took over as editor of the *Pall Mall Gazette*.

The magazine industry developed in a supporting role to the newspaper. Magazines provided more in-depth comment and discussion on stories and focused on human interest aspects. Magazines have always had a strong 'lifestyle' emphasis, reflecting trends in popular culture and entertainment.

Changing technology has had a profound influence on the periodical industry, with digitisation changing the way publications are produced, leading to 'rationalisation'. One of the most dramatic results of this in Britain was seen in 1986 when Rupert Murdoch's News International, owner of many leading titles, left its Fleet Street home for Wapping and significantly 'streamlined' its workforce.

'The nature of the industry has changed a lot in recent years. Management tends to be more draconian and there is a certain amount of insecurity, partly because of falling circulations. Technology has moved on and a lot of the traditional jobs have gone. Still, this has created new opportunities in other areas. It's important to keep up with the developments.'

Chief features sub-editor, regional newspaper

INTO THE FUTURE

The birth of choice

The broadcasting industry has until recently been relatively slow to change. After the launch of the BBC's television service in 1936, it was nearly 20 years before UK viewers had the option of another channel. It would be another 27 years before Channel 4 appeared on the scene, and a further 14 until Channel 5's arrival. It was not until 1967 that pro-grammes started to be broadcast in colour in this country, on the highly experimental BBC2. Even then it was initially only a few programmes, and it took some time for the idea to be fully accepted.

The 1980s were an important period in broadcasting's development, with interest developing in satellite and cable systems. Suddenly, a vast array of channels became available to the viewer. This came at a time when the government was emphasising the importance of consumer choice. This notion struck a chord with the British public, after so many years of only three channels.

The development of radio has been more consumer-led than television. Radio broadcasting is a much less complicated process, and it has long been possible to receive programmes from other parts of the world. It is also relatively easy for pirate broadcasters to get on the air. For this reason, listeners are more able to exercise choice, and the industry has had to meet their requirements. For instance, the popularity of Radio Luxembourg's music programmes forced the BBC to become more focused on popular music. Later, the success of pirate stations such as Radio Caroline, broadcasting from a boat off the English coast, resulted in the BBC launching Radio 1.

The broadcasting industry is now poised on the brink of some of the most dramatic changes in its history. These changes are driven by the communications revolution now underway and are likely to mean a closer relationship between all the different media.

Digital broadcasting

In digital broadcasting, the signal is sent as a code of ones and zeros, as opposed to the continuous wave of the analogue signal. Unlike analogue, the signal does not suffer from interference, resulting in clearer and more dependable pictures and sound. The digital signal takes up much less bandwidth and can be compressed, allowing many more channels to be broadcast with the existing mechanisms.

Digital is now accepted as the future of television broadcasting in this country. The BBC made a firm commitment to the technology some time ago – a necessary move for it to remain at the forefront of broadcasting. The advantages of digital prompted debate about whether the analogue signal should be shut down altogether. This now looks likely to happen. At the time of writing, Secretary of State for Culture, Media and Sport, Chris Smith, had just announced that a switch-off could be fully implemented as early as 2010 (providing broadcasters can promise to deliver digital through existing sets to 99.4% of the population).

TV and the Internet

The rise of the Internet has had a profound effect on the likely future of broadcasting. It is forecast that 50% of the population of western Europe will be using the Internet in ten years' time – a fact that broadcasters cannot afford to overlook. The Internet is now firmly established as a major communication medium. Its development has opened up previously undreamed of possibilities, and provided a view of how broadcasting may develop. The convergence of TV and the Internet is a media topic of the moment, and digital broadcasting paves the way for what Chris Smith recently described as 'the beginning of electronic communication as a seamless web transcending the old distinctions between television, computer and telephone'.

It is now possible for viewers to access the Internet, and all related services such as e-mail, through the television via a phone line and a set-top box. Viewers can watch TV and surf the net simultaneously. Internet and interactive TV has been available in the US for some time. The UK's first Internet and interactive TV service was launched in the UK by NTL in March 1999. A new generation of TV sets is in development that will be specially designed to enhance Internet use. This development could revolutionise the way people access information and services, and surveys indicate that take-up is likely to be high.

One of the most striking features of the Internet is that users can interact with it, and this benefit is now being brought to TV. Interactive services are starting to be offered by cable and satellite broadcasters in the UK and will become available from the BBC. Interactive programmes allow the viewer to get further information and services relating to the programme, to buy merchandise and to interact in other ways. Sport is a key area for interactivity, with viewers being able to choose camera angles and see action replays when they want.

Video on demand (VOD) is a dramatic prospect and will soon be widely available. VOD allows the viewer to choose when they want to watch a film or programme.

A technology revolution

'Rapidly advancing technology is having a dramatic effect on programme making. Camera technology has advanced phenomenally – the latest portable TV cameras are incredibly light and easy to use. One person can now go out and single-handedly shoot high-quality broadcast footage with sound.'

Camera operator

At the time of writing, this new technology was being pioneered in the UK by a London Weekend Television operation called The Lab. The Lab was founded because LWT needed to make programmes more cheaply. It makes a variety of programme types, including serious documentaries and entertainment shows. Its new way of making programmes is made possible by the easy-to-use equipment now available. The philosophy is of multi-skilling – one Lab worker can film a programme, operate the sound and lighting, and do the editing. The Lab is a very young culture – most workers are in their 20s. The Lab's approach is perhaps more obviously suited to reportage-style programmes, but they have successfully used it with other formats – including a studio show. Other companies are currently developing similar units.

As well as changes in the ways programmes are made, we could see some radical developments in broadcasting methods. Emerging broadband technologies will soon allow broadcast-quality images to be transmitted down phone lines. Potentially one person will be able to both make and broadcast a programme.

> 'The Internet could become a TV broadcasting mechanism in itself. Current restrictions include the limited amount of traffic websites can handle, but things change fast in cyberworld. Mainstream broadcasting seems fairly secure – for the time being anyway – but these developments could pave the way for a new generation of broadcasters.'
>
> *TV producer*

New directions in radio

The launch of digital satellite and cable services brought a degree of fear to the established radio industry, with the advent of CD-quality digital music channels catering for a variety of musical tastes. The industry is fairly robust though, and as a high proportion of listeners listen while driving, at work or otherwise out and about, such home-based systems are unlikely to replace radio as we know it.

Radio is perhaps more ideally suited to interaction with the Internet than TV. While TV is an all-engulfing medium that demands your full attention, you can listen to the radio while you do something else – like surfing the net. The two actually complement each other very well and a more truly interactive experience is possible than with TV. While listening you can explore links, find information on bands, music or gigs, and even see live pictures of bands and DJs in action.

Radio broadcasting via the Internet is gaining popularity, although poor bandwidth and expensive Internet access have hampered its full-scale explosion. This is set to change; broadband technology is developing rapidly, and the UK's first freephone service to the Internet became available in November 1999. During 1999, Internet giants such as Yahoo! and AOL began to invest heavily in developing radio services. The Internet allows even local broadcasters to reach listeners all over the world. The technology can even be extended to people on the move. Companies are experimenting with new technology to broadcast high-quality sound to mobile computers over the Internet.

Digital radio is also set to take off in a big way. It offers similar benefits to digital TV in that the sound is near CD quality and coverage is improved. To transmit FM radio to a large area using analogue requires a number of different frequencies for the same transmission. This is why you have to keep retuning your car radio to stay with the same station. Digital can cover a much wider area. Digital receivers are currently expensive but new chips now being developed will lead to significant price falls in the near future. Broadcasters (including the BBC and Virgin Radio) are investing heavily in digital radio services.

Printed media

Printed media remains a major world force. It is now evident that fears of the Internet imminently replacing newspapers and magazines, as well as books, were unfounded. However, the Internet revolution has hit the printed media sector too, and most major newspapers are now offering news and services online. The *Financial Times*'s website trebled its content during 1999. The majority of popular magazines have entertainment-based websites. These services are generally seen as complementing the printed material, or even extending its reach to new markets.

IT development is seen as a primary activity by the press and other news providers. Both the *Financial Times* and Reuters spend approximately 10% of their sales revenue on IT and research and development.

Although the papers will not become obsolete in the near future, the way news is distributed is likely to change. Digital photography is becoming more common – Reuters used exclusively digital images for its coverage of the 1998 World Cup. The images can be sent by phone or ISDN, which greatly reduces the time between taking a picture and publishing it.

What does it all mean for jobs?

The impact of rapidly changing technology on jobs in the media is hard to gauge. Over the years, the technological revolution has meant that many traditional jobs have disappeared. However, it has also led to the creation of jobs in new industry sectors. There are certainly concerns that the multi-skilled, low-personnel, low-cost TV production operations now being pioneered will dramatically reduce staff numbers. Technology will have an impact but will also create new opportunities. More companies will be making programmes, and it could become easier for people with talent but little or no experience to get jobs as much less training is required.

With new technology, considerably fewer people are needed to run a radio station. The take-off of Internet radio could actually provide a lot of opportunities for radio personnel with Internet skills, and for DJs and presenters. There is likely to be a proliferation of new stations, and great opportunities for expanding listenership and increasing advertising.

Newspapers and other traditional printed media remain extremely popular, and the market for 'lifestyle' and specialist magazines is still expanding. The jobs market is fairly stable, with increasing opportunities for those with IT skills.

The media industry is changing fast. One thing is for certain, however – communication is an ever more vital aspect of our world. The industry may shift in direction, but career opportunities are likely to increase.

WHO WORKS IN BROADCASTING?

There is a vast range of jobs in the broadcasting industry, in all aspects of pre-production, production, post-production, and the ever-expanding field of sales and marketing. Many jobs are highly specialised. It would not be possible to examine them all in a book such as this – it is essential that you do research of your own. However, we will look at a few jobs which are key roles in the process of making broadcast programmes.

Presenter

Presenters are at the high-profile end of broadcasting and can be the factor that determines a show's success or failure. Their actual involvement can vary considerably according to the nature of the programme. Presenters may well be involved in researching the programme and making editorial decisions about content and direction. Radio presenters, especially of music shows, are likely to have involvement in production. DJs usually operate much studio equipment themselves.

A related job is continuity announcing. Continuity announcers work in both radio and television, doing voice-overs that link programmes.

'A blend of skills is necessary these days – computer and technical skills are vital. There was a time when four people might work on a radio show – now it's often just one, doing all the different jobs, including the admin and paperwork. If you want to present, a good voice is important, as are interviewing skills – you may need to be persuasive to get what you want from people. A bit of ego helps to get you unscathed through live programmes, and you definitely need to be able to think on your feet. There's no easy route in – some people start as runners or production assistants and work their way up. This can take time and you may find yourself "typecast" in one of these roles. Journalism is worth considering as it gives you a lot of options.'

TV and radio presenter

This is not an easy career to plan for. Many presenters are recruited through having expertise or fame in a particular field, such as journalism or sport. Weather presenters are usually meteorologists. News readers are always broadcast journalists. There is no set way to become a presenter. You are unlikely to see the job advertised and it is often a case of being the right person in the right place at the right time. Personality and appearance are key factors (appearance is less important for radio presenters!). Voice training is common for people wanting to present and acting experience can be very useful.

If you are determined to become a presenter, get any kind of experience you can such as in hospital or college radio. If you're talented you may win through. There are courses available in TV and radio presenting. These certainly give no guarantee of getting work and can be costly, but you would at least get some (hopefully) well-produced demo footage to show around.

Essential qualities:
- strong personality
- good voice
- able to communicate with people of all kinds
- calm and controlled in a crisis
- unfazed when things don't go to plan
- able to ad lib
- able to cope with media attention.

Broadcast journalist

Broadcast journalists work in television and radio, and an increasing number are bi-media skilled, i.e. able to work in both fields. They work on a diverse range of programmes, finding news stories and turning them into the professional finished product that is presented to the public. They will generate story and programme ideas, carry out detailed research, interview people and report from locations. Some will edit and present their own material, and they may well be skilled in operating broadcasting equipment. Experienced broadcast journalists have a lot of responsibility for pro-gramme content.

Other journalists in this area include programme editors, who are responsible for the story content, order and emphasis of a programme, and correspondents, who report on specialist subject areas or locations.

Broadcast journalists will usually be educated to degree level and have a qualification in journalism. They will normally have experience as a journalist in newspapers, periodicals or local radio. Landing a job as a television researcher can be a good way for a journalist to move into television. Journalists often start out working on the bulletins desk in local radio, or in a local TV newsroom. A reputation for quality news brings prestige to TV companies, so they will be looking for the highest calibre people. Some companies, including the BBC, offer training schemes as a way in, but competition is extremely fierce. Journalism is one of the best ways into broadcasting if you don't want to start at the very bottom rung of the ladder.

Essential qualities:
- a feel for news
- knowledge of current affairs
- impartial and objective approach
- excellent communication skills
- on-camera presence
- writing flair
- able to remain calm in situations of panic and chaos.

Producer

There are producers in both television and radio. The exact nature of the job can vary dramatically depending on the nature of the programme, but essentially the producer is in charge of the show and involved in virtually every aspect of its production. The producer manages the budget and the people. They choose the production team, writers, actors etc., decide the show's content and production schedule, and oversee the whole process of getting it on air. In TV, producers work within a particular programme area, such as drama, comedy or news. They may be managing a number of projects at the same time and possibly a large number of staff. It is increasingly common to find producer-directors, who fulfil both roles.

A radio producer is likely to have considerable personal involvement, such as operating studio equipment and perhaps even presenting the show. They also manage the artistic side, creating the feel and tone of the programme – the role handled by the director in television.

As with many positions in broadcasting, there is no set route to becoming a producer. Producers are often graduates, although this is not a specific requirement. Would-be producers are expected to have several years' experience of programme-making and a knowledge of the disciplines involved. It won't be a first job. Producers often come from the technical professions, for example camera operators, and it can be a natural progression to a director, who is the key link between producer and production crew. Many producers have worked their way up, gaining hands-on experience of programme-making and discovering along the way a talent for organisation, managing people and budgetary control. If you're impatient and highly business-minded, you could try the alternative and increasingly common approach of setting up your own production company. Your business acumen rather than your production skills would be the crucial factor.

Essential qualities:
- full of programme ideas
- good manager
- excellent communicator
- able to control budgets
- long-term planning skills
- able to balance artistic and business needs
- presenting skills if appearing on air.

Director

Directors work in television and are responsible for the creative aspects of programme-making, determining the look and feel of the finished product. They work closely with the producer and often have involvement in programme planning, casting, script editing and choosing the production crew. As we have already mentioned, it is now common to find producer-directors, who do both jobs. The director co-ordinates the presenters, actors, camera, sound and lighting crews, etc., to achieve the result they want. They plan all the shots, camera angles and effects throughout the programme. Directors also oversee aspects of post-production, such as editing.

The most important requisites for a director are creative talent and an understanding of the whole production process. There are no set qualification requirements, and directors can, theoretically, start out in any aspect of production. It is fairly common for them to come from technical studio jobs, such as camera operator, and work their way up through the several assistant director ranks.

Director is a prestigious role which a great many people

aspire to, so there is a lot of competition and you will have to prove yourself continuously.

Another possible route in is through the non-broadcast industry, such as corporate and promotional films, or music videos. These kinds of productions tend to have much smaller teams, with more overlap of roles. It is, therefore, possible to gain directing skills in a shorter space of time. There are specific courses available, and many media courses cover aspects of directing. However, there is no substitute for hands-on experience. You can teach yourself a lot, and show your enthusiasm and determination, by making your own short films with a video camera.

Essential qualities:
- creative vision
- knowledge of production techniques
- able to communicate ideas to others
- good motivator
- able to interpret writers' intentions
- aware of budgetary restrictions.

Researcher

Researchers work in both TV and radio, playing a vital role in making programmes of all kinds. The job is seen as one of the best ways into the business, especially for those wanting to produce or direct. The researcher will use a wide range of information sources, such as libraries, archives, companies, individuals and the Internet, to research information relevant to the programme and ensure broadcast material is factually correct. They are very involved with people, screening guests for shows and researching their career or background, tracking down experts and persuading people to appear.

Researchers may be involved in generating the original ideas for programmes. Although the job can have its glamorous aspects – lucky researchers may be sent on location abroad – there is a lot of drudgery. Hours of work can be long and contracts are usually short. Researchers in radio are fewer now because of the reduced staffing structures; much of this work is often done by the producer. They have a production assistant role and do other tasks as required, such as manning phone lines.

Because this job is seen as a good way in, competition is stiff. Once in, you will have to prove yourself continuously. However, researchers who are personable and make the production go smoothly will get more work. Most researchers are graduates. Relevant experience, such as some form of journalism or research in another field, is very useful. Broadcasting experience of any kind will definitely help, and volunteering for unpaid work may help you get the right experience.

Research jobs tend not to be advertised, often arising quickly and being filled by word of mouth. Keep writing to TV companies or radio stations (without making a nuisance of yourself) and you might get lucky, especially if you have specialist knowledge in a particular area.

Essential qualities:
- well-organised
- attention to detail
- excellent people skills
- knowledge of information sources
- diligent and resourceful
- IT skills.

Editor

Editors work in television. Theirs is perhaps the most important role in post-production. The editor has a significant input into the overall look and feel of the programme, linking the scenes together to get the right flow and order, and ensuring that sound and picture for film are perfectly matched (these record simultaneously on video). The editor makes decisions as to which scenes need to be removed and must sometimes find very creative solutions to link scenes appropriately. Most editing is done on videotape using computer software such as Lightworks and Avid. Some high-quality productions still use film, with individual frames having to be physically cut out and the film stuck back together.

Good editing can cover up a multitude of sins committed

by directors, actors or presenters. Editors often spend a lot of time in editing suites, alone or with an assistant. Some, if working on live broadcasts such as news reports, may be out on location.

Many editors are film or media graduates, and most will be educated at least to A level standard. The majority are taken on by companies as assistants or trainees – some experience of production is often required. Other technical professionals, such as vision mixers, can move up to the role of editor. Getting some editing experience is vital. Get a video or Super-8 camera and some basic editing equipment, and start using it! Or join a club or community group that will give you access to video equipment. Basically, just get as much experience as you can and try to develop your creative feel for editing. Make a 'showreel', i.e. a tape of material you've edited, to show to people.

You could try to get experience by assisting a freelance editor, especially if you've got some relevant knowledge. They often advertise in trade journals such as *Broadcast* – try writing to a few.

Essential qualities:
- creativity
- understanding of how cuts will look
- attention to detail
- good visual and colour sense
- well-organised
- understanding of the material and the director's requirements
- computer skills.

Camera operator

The camera operator (no longer a cameraman) is perhaps the job that immediately springs to mind when you think about the TV industry. It is their work that makes the whole business possible. Camera operators work under instruction from the director to get the shots and effect he or she requires. The task is more creative than it might sound, however, as the camera operator must interpret what the director is trying to convey and know how to get exactly the right artistic effect. An experienced camera operator may plan shots with the director, especially if they work together regularly. Camera work can be a good way into directing.

Camera operators are often studio-based but may also work on location. They may be required to film in all weathers and possibly difficult, or even dangerous, circumstances – news camera crews can find themselves in the middle of wars and natural disasters. Camera operators are often expected to maintain their equipment, rig it up and transport it around. Freelancers may be expected to provide their own equipment. Working hours can be long.

Many camera operators have degrees or HNDs, although this is not a strict requirement. Technical subjects such as computing or electronics are likely to be useful. Most media and TV courses will give you the opportunity to specialise in camera work. If you want to be a camera operator you will probably already be into photography, and this is a good way to develop your aptitude for TV camera work.

Getting as much experience as you can is vital. Get a video camera and start making your own films. Join clubs and societies and learn everything you can from people with any skill. Work on your still photography, too. Camera operators often start out as camera assistants or technical

'Any experience you can get of making programmes or being involved in some way shows employers that you have a real interest and enthusiasm – this counts for a lot. I came across a number of people who had been in the same university TV society as me working for the BBC and other TV companies. There are plenty of community video and broadcasting associations that you can get involved in. Even just being a keen photographer could be useful. Putting together some sort of showreel is definitely a good idea. A lot of camera people start off maybe as runners or technicians. You may have to pester people to help you get the skills you want. If you prove yourself to be keen and able, you could perhaps move up to be second camera assistant and work your way up from there.'

Camera operator

trainees. TV companies, including the BBC and ITV, offer traineeships. Places are limited and competition is fierce.

Essential qualities:
- good at following instructions
- able to interpret what the director wants
- excellent understanding of the material
- sound technical knowledge
- understanding of the whole production process
- passion for photography.

Vision mixer

Vision mixers work in television. The job is related to editing, but vision mixers work on programmes going out live or being recorded. They cut from one camera to another according to the director's instructions and link into other items such as live transmissions via satellite, pre-recorded video clips or graphics. Vision may well be mixed in time to music, as with live music shows. The vision mixer works in the control room along with the director and producer. Opportunities are decreasing as directors increasingly handle this work themselves. Also, bear in mind that this can be a stressful job as your work may be going out live to millions of people.

There are no formal qualification requirements for vision mixers. They are usually recruited internally, either from technical staff or from admin staff with some production experience, and would probably begin as an assistant or trainee. A media production qualification of some sort could well be useful. In fact, many media courses will give you experience of vision mixing.

Essential qualities:
- excellent visual sense
- great timing and co-ordination
- calm under pressure
- technical aptitude
- good grasp of overall programme concepts
- musical knowledge is useful.

Production assistant

PAs work in both TV and radio. The role is extremely diverse and involves contact with virtually every area of production. In a nutshell, the PA is assistant to the producer and/or director, and provides the main point of contact between them and the crew. They will be involved in the making of a programme from the outset to the very end. They are the organisers and the 'fixers', setting up production meetings, arranging and rearranging production schedules, making sure everyone is at the right place at the right time and with the right equipment, and solving problems of all kinds.

PAs are responsible for administering the programme's budget, sorting out payments, and many other aspects of administration. They may well have a research role, especially if there isn't a dedicated researcher on the show. They will often meet and greet guests, link between director and camera during filming, and be involved in the editing process. This is a demanding and often stressful job, but PAs can get experience in virtually every aspect of the business.

A PA job is often a step up for someone working as a secretary in broadcasting, or for a runner. PAs are often graduates, although this is not a specific requirement.

Getting any kind of broadcasting experience should be your first step. Would-be PAs are often expected to have some knowledge of production techniques, so learn as much as you can. It is possible to get in on a trainee scheme. As with many such schemes there is a lot of competition, and previous practical experience is increasingly expected.

Essential qualities:
- well-organised
- administrative and computer skills
- good at accounting and budgeting
- excellent communication skills
- sound understanding of production
- calm in a crisis
- energy and enthusiasm.

Runner

Runners work in television. This job is the classic entry-level position. It is the bottom rung on the ladder, but can potentially lead anywhere for talented people prepared to work their way up. A runner is essentially a 'gofer'. Their job is to do virtually anything that anyone in the production department demands. This can include administration tasks, delivering film and video, travel booking, passing on messages, helping with studio equipment, and (frequently) making tea. Runners often put in very long hours. The job can be very hectic, with never-ending requests and demands from every quarter.

Runners are often media graduates seeking to break into the business. Many runners work for free to gain experience of the industry, or for a very low wage. The best approach is to write to companies with your CV. If you have a strong interest in an area such as documentary making or drama, try targeting the companies or departments that make these programmes. Make sure you convey your enthusiasm and any relevant experience or knowledge. Be patient and stick with it.

Essential qualities:
- energy and motivation
- a passion for TV work
- willingness to learn
- adaptability
- admin and computer skills
- well-organised
- able to use your initiative.

Media sales executive

Media sales executives sell advertising space in television, radio and new media areas such as websites. The job involves dealing with existing customers and generating new business.

Media sales executives are usually office-based and often spend a good proportion of their day on the phone. There may also be face-to-face contact with customers.

There are no specific entry requirements, but a successful track record in some form of sales is likely to be required. Media experience is not a prerequisite. Some companies will take on trainees with or without experience.

There may be no particular qualification requirements, especially if you have experience in selling or a relevant aspect of customer service. However, many companies prefer to recruit graduates. Those with aptitude can progress quickly into team leader and management roles.

Essential qualities:
- drive and determination
- a knowledge of sales techniques
- good communication skills
- confidence
- negotiating skills
- ability to think on your feet.

MYTH BUSTER

Land a job in TV and you're half-way to being a star

Becoming a TV personality is a very hit-and-miss affair. There are plenty of talented people out there who don't make it. Being in a broadcasting environment can be a good way to get experience, but you are unlikely to become even slightly famous without a good deal of luck.

BROADCASTING – WHERE ARE THE JOBS?

The TV industry

When you think about a career in TV, who do you visualise working for? Most people will automatically think of big names such as the BBC and ITV. Although these companies are substantial employers, a large number of the shows you see on TV are not actually made by the companies that broadcast them. The major TV companies are known as publisher/ broadcasters because a proportion of their programming is commissioned from other companies. A wide variety of independent service providers are likely to have been involved in the process of bringing a show to your screen.

Independent production companies

Following the 1990 Broadcasting Act, a quarter of all the programmes broadcast by a TV company must come from independent producers. The Act had the effect of instantly creating quite a large industry sector. These companies, often very small outfits with few permanent employees, are where many people begin their broadcasting careers. Independents produce programmes of all types. Some make programmes in a variety of genres although many, particularly the smaller ones, are likely to specialise.

Most people who want to get into the industry are excited by the prospect of working on broadcast TV programmes. The reality of life in independent production, however, is that a good deal of the sector's revenue comes from less glamorous projects, such as corporate productions, training videos and commercials.

Be that as it may, independents can offer very good opportunities. They are generally easier to get into and, because of their smaller size, talented people will be noticed. You will probably get the opportunity to become multiskilled as staff often have to fulfil more than one role.

Working at a small independent, possibly on a voluntary basis, is a good way to try out a few different areas of work to see what you like doing and have an aptitude for.

Facilities companies

Because most independent production companies tend to be small operations, they are unlikely to have much in the way of facilities and resources. They probably won't have a studio, and the staff is likely to be minimal. The nature of the TV industry is that there are very different requirements for different programmes. Programme makers will, therefore, buy in the specialist services of other independent operators, the facilities companies, as and when they need them. Facilities companies are another area where many people get their first industry experience and become skilled.

Commercial studios will often provide the studio and equipment such as cameras and lighting. They may also provide the people, including camera operators, lighting and sound engineers, other technical staff, and even admin staff.

Outside broadcast companies are another specialist service. They provide the facilities, including equipment and people, needed to record, or broadcast live, events taking place away from the studio.

Post-production is also frequently handled by independent companies. They may handle editing, graphics and other specialised services such as dubbing and effects.

The BBC

With around 23,000 employees, the BBC is the largest single employer in the industry. The BBC makes many of its own programmes and broadcasts globally via the World Service. The BBC is currently funded by the TV licence fee. It is managed by a board of governors, headed by the Director General (currently Greg Dyke).

The BBC is perhaps the organisation that most people interested in a broadcasting career aspire to work for. There are good reasons for this – its programme making and news are respected worldwide, and training and development opportunities within the organisation are excellent.

There are opportunities at the BBC across the spectrum of jobs, with multimedia being a major growth area. The BBC is increasingly moving towards a recruitment system where applicants' skills are logged and matched to opportunities as they arise.

ITV

The Independent Television companies are a federation of licensed regional broadcasters which together achieve national coverage. There are 15 ITV licence holders, covering 14 regional broadcasting areas (there are two licences for London). The ITV companies are actually owned by quite a small number of organisations. At the time of writing, a merger was planned between two of them, the success of which would mean the bulk of ownership being divided between two parent companies. The ITV companies are funded by advertising revenue and sponsorship.

Some of the ITV companies, particularly the older ones, make their own programmes. The newer ones are more likely to buy them in from independents and other ITV companies. The trend away from programme making has meant a reduction in employee numbers, with freelance and short contract staff being brought in as needed.

ITN
Independent Television News is the company designated by the ITC to supply news programmes to the ITV companies. Revenue comes from selling its programmes to these companies and others, including Channel 4. ITN has its own studios and employs broadcast personnel and journalists.

Channel 4 and S4C
Channel 4 and S4C (the Welsh 4th channel) are both funded by advertising revenue. Neither company makes any programmes itself. Staff levels are comparatively low at both companies and there are obviously no jobs related to programme making. The main areas of employment are sales and marketing and technical/engineering professions.

Channel 5
Channel 5, Britain's newest channel, is funded by advertising revenue. Like Channel 4, it does not make its own programmes and has relatively low staff levels.

Satellite and cable companies
Satellite and cable companies are funded partly through advertising revenue and partly through viewer subscriptions. The largest of these companies in the UK is British Sky Broadcasting (BSkyB). Much of these companies' programming is bought in, although some do make their own programmes. A growth area for jobs with these companies is in interactive and multimedia production. Other key recruitment areas are sales and marketing and technical/engineering.

'Working in a small company means you have to muck in with the team – everybody has to take a turn at the less exciting jobs. The great thing is you get to try your hand at everything – I've done camera work, editing and even a bit of directing. The money's not great, but if you're good your ability is more likely to be recognised – you're not just a small cog in a big machine.'

Production company assistant

The radio industry

Radio in this country has been dominated by the BBC for even longer than the TV industry. However, commercial radio is now on the increase and the number of independent production companies is growing.

Although expanding, radio is a comparatively small industry. It is also much less labour-intensive than TV since two or three people can be enough to get a programme on the air. Jobs are, therefore, not that plentiful.

The BBC

The BBC operates five national radio stations and a network of regional stations, and is the largest single employer in the radio industry. As with the television service, funding comes from the licence fee.

The full range of radio jobs can be found at the BBC. There is an increasing trend towards bi-media skilling and some BBC employees – journalists in particular – may be expected to work in both radio and television.

Commercial radio

The commercial radio sector has consistently expanded since its legalisation in 1973. Funding is through advertising revenue. This fact, coupled with the relatively small workforce size at commercial radio stations, means that all employees need to be fairly commercially aware. The range of jobs is broadly the same as at the BBC, although commercial stations tend not to make so many labour-intensive factual programmes, so jobs such as dedicated researchers are less common. There are, however, more opportunities in marketing and sales.

Independent production companies

The independent sector is a small but growing industry area. As with the TV industry, independent production companies make programmes, which are bought by commercial radio stations or the BBC. They usually obtain a contract for a particular time slot and bring in freelance or contract staff to make the programme. As the sector grows, this may well become a good area for people to get a start in radio.

Hospital radio

Hospital radio has been known for being the classic route into the industry – many famous radio personalities started out this way. It is a public service, providing entertainment to hospital patients. Hospital radio is staffed by volunteers. Working in hospital radio is not a career but can be a valuable way to gain much-needed experience.

Community radio

The community radio sector is a diverse network of local projects and groups united by the Community Media Association. They are usually funded through a combination of community and government grants, advertising revenue and sponsorship. As with hospital radio, this sector is largely operated by volunteers. Most community projects have a commitment to training volunteers in broadcasting skills, so again this can be a good way to get experience.

WHO WORKS IN PRINTED MEDIA?

'Words are things and a small drop of ink
Falling like dew, upon a thought, produces
That which makes thousands, perhaps millions think.'
Lord Byron (1788–1824)

Many of the jobs available in newspapers and magazines fall under the broad heading of 'journalism'. This term incorporates a range of jobs which can be quite different in nature. In this section, we will look at some of the key roles in the production of printed publications. All these jobs are commonly done on a freelance basis.

Reporter

Reporters find, research and write stories for newspapers and other publications. The job can involve being sent to all kinds of locations – some not too glamorous – at any time of the day or night to cover a story. A good reporter will be able to create an interesting piece even on a topic that may appear quite dull. Good reporters use interviewing skills to get insightful views on the story. Reporters may cover specialist areas such as technology, business or finance. Many are freelance.

There are two main routes into journalism. Some people may get on to a training programme or Modern Apprenticeship with a particular publication. This is called 'direct entry'.

These days, the 'pre-entry' route is more common – journalists are recruited after completing vocational courses for journalism accredited by the National Council for the Training of Journalists (NCTJ). The vast majority of entrants to the profession are now graduates with a recognised postgraduate qualification in journalism.

Qualifications alone will not get you a job – you will have to demonstrate your skill and commitment to an editor. Experience of working on a student newspaper or similar will certainly help. It is definitely worth submitting articles for publication in local papers and the free press. A portfolio including some press clippings will give you valuable added credibility.

Essential qualities:
- excellent writing skills
- determined and tenacious
- interviewing and people skills
- able to see the story angle in any situation
- strong interest in current affairs
- an interest in the community
- able to work to deadlines and under pressure
- willingness to work unsociable hours.

Features writer

The features writer's role is often less news-based than that of most journalists. They write features – i.e. in-depth articles – on a range of subjects. Some will specialise in a particular area such as fashion, sport or politics. Features writers work for a wide variety of publications, particularly newspapers and magazines. Many work freelance. Writers may be commissioned for one-off pieces or may get a regular slot.

A features writer can progress to features editor. This is a role which involves commissioning writers and editing their work, managing a team and decision-making.

> 'Freelances are central to the industry – there is plenty of work out there, it's just a question of taking the bull by the horns and having the confidence to sell yourself and your ideas to editors. A lot of the work you do may be fairly mundane – bread-and-butter stuff – but even this can lead to more interesting spin-offs. I write on property for one magazine. Through this connection I have been able to start doing travel pieces, which is great fun. You have to adapt to what is marketable. I love writing environmental features but could not make a living just from this.'
>
> *Freelance features writer*

Unlike many journalistic roles, a qualification in journalism is not necessarily a requirement for features writers. However, the majority probably do come from a journalistic background. A proven track record of writing is certainly a requirement – you will not be taken seriously if you have nothing in print. Submitting articles for publication in the free press, student newspapers and local papers is a good start. You can also write features on topical subjects and submit them to local and national newspapers and magazines. Most will pay per article, based on the number of words. If what you have written meets their needs you may get lucky. There is a lot of skill in gauging what articles particular publications will be interested in and tailoring your style to the readership. Making good connections is very important and you will need to publicise yourself extensively at first. Get as much experience as you can and hone your writing and editing skills. A good portfolio is essential.

Essential requirements:
- excellent command of English and grammar
- engaging writing style
- able to adapt style to different audiences
- excellent communication skills
- able to work to deadlines and under pressure
- in-depth knowledge of subject area
- research skills
- computer literacy.

Sub-editor

Sub-editors work on newspapers, magazines and other publications, and are responsible for the final look and content of the publication. They will rewrite and 'tweak' the copy to ensure it reads well, and may edit stories to a shorter length. Sub-editors arrange the layout of text and images on the page, and write headlines and picture captions. An important aspect of the job is ensuring facts are checked and that everything fits into the house style. Sub-editors will liaise closely with reporters, writers and editors.

'I manage the department and have overall responsibility for the content and look of the features pages. The work of a sub-editor involves revising and checking the copy, rewriting articles, writing headlines, laying out the pages and chasing up photos. We are generally ensuring the end product is well-designed, that everything that should be there is there, and that it goes out on time – a very important factor. You need to be creative, but also fast, accurate and disciplined. Language and writing skills are essential. A strong interest in news and a good knowledge of current affairs is important. Adaptability and a relaxed attitude will help you deal with any unexpected problems that crop up.'
Chief features sub-editor, regional newspaper

Newspaper sub-editors usually come from a journalistic background, probably starting out as a reporter, so this is unlikely to be a first job. Magazine sub-editors often come from journalism, although other backgrounds, such as graphic design, copywriting and book publishing, are also common.

Experience of writing is a usual requirement, as are IT skills and knowledge of desktop publishing packages such as QuarkXPress. Although many in this profession are graduates, a degree is not a specific requirement. However, those wanting to work in the newspaper industry are likely to need a degree and a postgraduate qualification in journalism.

Essential requirements:
- excellent knowledge of English language and grammar
- good writing skills
- able to see the important points in an article
- accuracy and eye for detail
- communication skills
- able to work to deadlines and under pressure
- knowledge of current affairs.

Picture researcher

Picture researchers work on all manner of publications, including newspapers and magazines, and also in the TV and film industries. Their function is to source and obtain pictures for use in a publication. A picture researcher will be briefed on the type of image required and will do extensive research to find the best match. They will build up an extensive network of contacts, including picture libraries, archives, collections and other sources. The picture researcher is responsible for negotiating and arranging fees, resolving copyright issues and ensuring sources are credited. They may well be involved in checking and ensuring print quality. An important part of the job is keeping detailed records of all transactions and keeping on top of financial and legal issues. A picture researcher can move on to become a picture editor or manager – a role with more responsibility for managing staff and contracts.

A degree is not always a specific requirement but will certainly increase your prospects. A picture researcher may start out as a picture research assistant. Experience of working in a picture library or in publishing is very useful. Some experience of photography, if only in an amateur capacity, is likely to be expected, as is some knowledge of art. Foreign language skills are also very helpful as pictures may have to be sourced from abroad. Short courses in picture research are available and could be useful in combination with some appropriate work experience. There are occasionally opportunities to enter as a trainee with a particular organisation, but these are hard to come by.

Essential qualities:
- good artistic and visual sense
- research skills
- IT skills
- persistence and determination
- good communication skills
- financial awareness
- able to work to budgets and deadlines
- understanding of legal issues
- methodical and well-organised.

Press photographer/photojournalist

Press photographers work mainly for newspapers and magazines, press agencies and photo agencies. Other employers may include TV companies. Freelance work is more common than permanent employment these days. The role of the press photographer is to capture striking images of news and events for publication. Some specialise in one area, such as celebrities, fashion or sports. Freelance photographers will be commissioned to cover an event. Alternatively, they may decide independently what to cover, and then try to sell the pictures afterwards. Photographers commonly work unpredictable hours. Photojournalists are bi-skilled, both reporting stories and doing the photography.

It is not easy to get work as a press photographer. Most have qualifications in photography, commonly to degree level. You will be expected to have experience and a good portfolio of work. Networking and self-promotion are very important for getting work. When starting out you will need to show your work to as many people as possible. Photo agencies are probably a good start. It may take quite some time to get any response, even if your work is good. Once you do get work, if you prove competent and reliable more will probably follow. There are a lot of other people trying to make it in this profession, so you will need to be constantly chasing opportunities and making connections. Training in both photography and journalism is a good way of making yourself more employable.

Essential qualities:
- reliability
- photographic skill and an eye for a great shot
- able to anticipate events/stories to cover
- motivated and determined
- strong interest in current affairs
- willing to work unsociable hours
- understanding of a client or editor's needs.

Graphic designer

Graphic designers work on publications of all kinds, including newspapers and magazines. In smaller publications, the graphic designer will be responsible for the layout and presentation of the whole publication. On a newspaper or large magazine, they are more likely to be doing advertising design, information graphics and illustrations of various kinds. Graphic designers work with text and images to create the right visual impact for the publication, and meet the needs of the client. The designer works to a brief from the client. Sometimes there is scope for considerable artistic freedom, sometimes a strict formula must be followed. Graphic design is now more or less entirely done on computer – Apple Mac is the industry standard. Designers need to keep abreast of new software and technological developments.

'Although being able to draw is not necessarily an essential requirement for people working in graphics these days, it is certainly a big help. You need a good visual sense and sense of colour. Being able to visualise things in 3D is important for information graphics. An interest in current affairs is quite important – you need to know the relative importance of news stories and keep yourself up-to-date with what's happening in the world. Most graphics work is done on computer so it's essential to have a certain level of IT knowledge. Keeping up with new developments enables you to be more creative and progressive in the kinds of graphics you produce.'

Chief graphic artist, regional newspaper

A degree is not a specific requirement for many employers. However, a degree, HND or BTEC in a relevant subject, such as graphic design, photography or art, will be a great help. The most important thing is to demonstrate design flair and a knowledge of the relevant desktop publishing software such as QuarkXPress, Adobe Photoshop, Adobe Illustrator, Freehand, and Corel Draw. Reasonable competence in some or all of these is likely to be expected for a job at any level. There are many part-time and short courses available. If you have access to a computer and software at home, you can teach yourself a great deal. Tutorial packages are widely available – even over the Internet. It is very important to have a good portfolio. You need to put a lot of work into making this as professional as you can because it shows employers what you are capable of. Getting some work experience will be very valuable. You may be able to get a placement at a design studio. Even if you have to do this on an unpaid basis, it will help you get the experience you need.

Essential qualities:
- visual sense and design flair
- knowledge of design software
- able to interpret a brief
- good communication skills
- able to work to deadlines and under pressure
- willing to work extra hours when necessary
- problem-solving skills.

Media sales executive

Media sales executives sell advertising space in newspapers, magazines and other publications. As in broadcasting, the job involves dealing with existing customers and generating new business. Media sales executives are usually office based and often spend a good part of their day on the phone. There may also be face-to-face contact with customers.

There are no specific entry requirements, but a successful track record in some form of sales is usually required. Previous media experience is not necessary. Some companies take on trainees with or without experience.

There may be no particular qualification requirements, especially if you have experience in selling or a relevant aspect of customer service. However, many companies prefer to recruit graduates. Those with aptitude can progress into team leader and management roles.

Essential qualities:
- drive and determination
- a knowledge of sales techniques
- good communication skills
- confidence
- negotiating skills
- ability to think on your feet.

MYTH BUSTER

Journalism is a glamorous profession

As an emerging journalist you are unlikely to be interviewing celebrities and mixing with the rich and famous. The majority of journalists are working on trade, business and financial publications or local papers.

PRINTED MEDIA – WHERE ARE THE JOBS?

Although staffing levels have fallen in some areas, notably daily newspapers, opportunities have arisen in new areas. Newspapers are a stable, if not expanding, sector. Established respectability is an important factor, making it very difficult to establish a new paper.

National newspapers

Most of the national daily papers are based in London, a notable exception being *The Guardian*, which is in Manchester. They fall into two main categories: broadsheets and tabloids. Increasingly, papers are not independent operations but owned by large syndicates such as Rupert Murdoch's News International and the late Robert Maxwell's Mirror Group. Many people in or seeking journalistic positions aspire to work for the dailies because of the higher-impact news and better wages. There is an increasing trend towards outsourcing printing operations, so jobs related to this are not offered by the paper itself.

Local newspapers

Local papers are where the majority of people in the industry cut their teeth. It is very hard to get into the nationals without experience so this is a good starting point. Most towns and cities will have at least one local paper so work can probably be found close to home. Some local papers have an excellent reputation for the quality of their journalism – local does not necessarily mean inferior.

The free press

Free local papers are to be found all over the country. They are distributed free and funded by advertising revenue. Although they don't have the prestige of a regular local paper, working for a free paper can be a good way to get experience. These operations are usually very small so pay is likely to be minimal.

Student newspapers

The student rag is the classic starting point for a journalistic career, where media wannabes are able to get hands-on experience of working on a newspaper. Small-scale operations such as these can give students the opportunity to experience a variety of journalistic and editorial roles.

Magazines

Magazines are a growth industry. Established magazines are reasonably stable and new ones starting up have a reasonable success rate considering the number of competitors. The growth of the industry has been linked to the strength of the economy and the amount of disposable income that people have. Lifestyle magazines are a current trend which seems to be growing in popularity. Special interest magazines are springing up to cover virtually every subject under the sun and these can be a good starting point for your career.

Trade publications

A significant proportion of journalists work in the 'unseen' sector of trade publications. Many now get their journalistic grounding in this way. Every industry, however obscure, is covered by at least one trade publication – from insurance to textile manufacturing to drain inspection. This may not be the most glamorous end of the media but it is certainly a growing employment sector. Increasing numbers of people who want to get into any aspect of journalism are likely to find themselves working on trade publications at some stage in their career.

Newsletters and small publications

The development of easy-to-use desktop publishing software has led to a rapid growth in newsletters and other small-circulation publications. Small capacity printing operations have sprung up across the country in response to demand. The decreasing cost of producing a publication means that this trend is likely to continue. Although the operations are small, the growing numbers mean that media work opportunities are increasing.

'Business journalism may not be the most glamorous end of the profession, but it is certainly a good way to learn your trade. The advantage of working for small publications is that you get to try your hand at subbing, page layout and design, etc. – all useful skills that will help further your career. You have more input into the overall feel of the publication.'

Journalist

ELECTRONIC MEDIA

> 'Neither a wise man or a brave man lies down on the tracks of history to wait for the train of the future to run over him.'
> Dwight D. Eisenhower (1890–1969), 37th US President

We are living in times where information and its rapid delivery are ever more important. As global trading becomes more common, businesses are increasingly reliant on information being up to the minute and instantly available. The way that information is stored and accessed has also been radically affected with the advent of the CD-ROM. New forms of media are evolving fast. Some, such as the CD-ROM, have become commonplace in quite a short space of time. Electronic media is a very exciting area because it is developing so fast and so radically. Don't blink!

Online media

Services to business are among the fastest-growing areas in the development of the Internet, and a purpose to which it is ideally suited. Many new and established companies are providing online information services, including news, financial data and market reports. These services are becoming increasingly interactive. Bloomberg is now operating an interactive news service for journalists and businesses. Users have access to services including live and archived video, news in text form, reports and market data, available 24 hours a day. The days of waiting until tomorrow (to read it in the newspaper) are well and truly over.

Online services are being provided by established companies, such as Bloomberg and the *Financial Times*, to extend their existing reach. There are also many new companies that are exclusively Internet based. Many have sprung up to cater for highly specialised information needs.

Automated publishing is a new area that may well affect the way information is accessed. A key technique is 'object orientation'. An object such as a picture or news article is intelligently coded so that it places itself according to given criteria. This means publications could effectively write themselves and be generated to match the specific information requirements of an organisation or individual. The techniques could be applied to either online or printed publications.

The way people access online media is set to change. Many more people are likely to access the Internet through their TVs and palmtop computers in the near future. Wireless Application Protocol (WAP)-enabled mobile phones can now be used to access certain websites – for instance, browsing the ITN news headlines. There are already more mobile phones than PCs in this country, and it has been predicted that there will be more mobiles than TVs by the year 2004. This could have a major impact on the future of online media.

'The Internet has a lot of advantages over other media for delivering news coverage. On TV or radio you may only have a short slot in which to report a story. On the Internet your coverage can be much more in-depth and can include real video and audio footage, live interviews, text pieces, and analysis. The scope for enhancing the coverage provided through other media is enormous.'

Online news co-ordinator

Who hasn't got a website?

These days it is hard to find a company that doesn't have a presence on the web. Some websites are a token gesture to the information age, but increasing numbers of companies use their website to generate business and to reach new markets. Websites are now much more than just a way for companies to advertise their services – they are becoming an entire media form. With new sound and vision capabilities emerging, websites are becoming more and more like broadcasting stations. However, website technology is still far ahead of broadcasting in terms of interactivity.

Multimedia

Multimedia brings together text, sound, pictures and animation. Its emergence as an important media form has been made possible by the Internet and CD-ROM technology. Websites and CD-ROMs commonly use this technology to make their content more dynamic and appealing to users and to bring a new dimension of interactivity to publications. Multimedia applications are becoming more widespread. Companies are starting to use multimedia packages to train staff. Publications such as encyclopaedias, information listings, prospectuses and educational resources are now available in multimedia format on CD-ROM.

Media storage technology

The CD-ROM is now firmly established as one of the most important storage media. CD-ROMs are small, lightweight and capable of holding large volumes of information. Multi-volume publications can now be contained on CD-ROM and accessed extremely easily. What's more, a CD-ROM can be networked on a computer system so the information can be accessed by many users simultaneously.

New developments in CD-ROM technology include business card-sized CD-ROMs. Companies are now starting to use these to promote their business. These small CDs can hold impressive multimedia presentations and link to a company's website for further information and updates. Costs are continually falling so it may only be a matter of time before we start to see newspapers and magazines, especially the weekly and monthly ones, being offered in this format. As handheld computers become smaller and more powerful the demand for this may grow.

Digital versatile disk (DVD) is an emerging technology that may have a large impact on the media. High-quality film and video pictures can be stored on these – an entire motion picture will fit on one disk.

WHO WORKS IN ELECTRONIC MEDIA?

The pace of development in the world of electronic media makes it difficult to pin down actual jobs in the industry since roles and skill requirements are changing rapidly. Job titles can be misleading – a job description for the same title can vary enormously between different companies. Salaries can also differ hugely. Qualification requirements are also difficult to comment on. Formal qualifications tend to be less important in this industry. Skills, particularly transferable skills, are of prime importance. We can, however, look at some of the broader areas in which people work...

Journalistic and content provider roles

Online services use journalists, writers and editors to create the content and keep it up to date. They can be an excellent starting point for newly qualified journalists. Writers and commentators on many different subject areas are also employed, as are copy editors or sub-editors. A good knowledge of computers and relevant software is usually required. A basic knowledge of HTML can be a big help in getting work.

Designer

The designer's role is very important in the electronic media industry. Multimedia designers work on websites and an ever-increasing range of interactive applications. A graphic design background is usual and a thorough knowledge of software is essential. Skill in 3D-design applications such as CAD are becoming more important. A combination of design flair and technological competence is required.

Developer

Developers work on the creation of the whole application or project, bringing together all the different technical and artistic elements. The key function is to ensure the application fully satisfies what is demanded of it. This role requires the ability to see the whole picture and get all involved parties working together.

Producer

Rather like the corresponding role in TV or radio, multimedia producers organise the production process, manage staff and budgets and negotiate contracts. Strong managerial skills as well as technical knowledge are required.

Programmer

Programmers are essential in making the project happen. As well as having in-depth knowledge of relevant programming languages, they need to be creative thinkers – programming must support both the artistic and technical needs of the project. Problem-solving skills are an important attribute.

ELECTRONIC MEDIA – WHERE ARE THE JOBS?

The majority of people in the industry work for specialist companies. These include Internet Service Providers (ISPs), online news and information services and multimedia companies. Many of these are small companies with few employees. Multimedia is becoming so widespread that jobs are now to be found in many different areas of industry, and in both the private and public sectors.

> 'Business is becoming turned on to e-commerce, and multimedia presentations and promotions are now common practice for companies. It is usual for companies to buy these services from specialist providers. However, increasing numbers – particularly among larger companies – now have their own multimedia and Internet departments. The corporate sector is becoming a major multimedia employer.'
>
> *Multimedia developer, international software company*

Television is set to become a major boom area. Websites are already becoming important to broadcasting companies. The BBC is a prime example. Its website supports many aspects of the BBC's programming and educational provision. As interactive TV takes off, many more opportunities will be created for people with appropriate skills.

Newspapers and magazines are another growth area. Many now have a web presence and interactive services are increasing in importance.

ELECTRONIC MEDIA SKILLS

The fast-changing nature of the industry makes it difficult to pin down specific skill requirements for jobs – new and different skills may be needed six months down the line.

Electronic media is an area where skills need to be updated on an ongoing basis to keep up with industry needs. Most employers look for transferable skills, generic skills that can be applied in lots of different situations, enabling people to cope with a changing job description.

Teamworking

Working effectively as a member of a team is vital in every electronic media area. The industry is very much team-orientated. People with different specialities work closely together to create a unified solution or particular product. Each member's contribution is equally important. This is a situation where the whole is greater than the sum of its parts.

Project work

Work in electronic media tends to be project-based, so people need to have a grasp of the bigger picture and how their role fits into it. Workers need to be able to see the project through its different stages and adapt accordingly. Experience of project management, planning and organisation is very valuable.

Learning skills and adaptability

The ability to learn effectively is a skill in itself. In this industry it is essential to be able to learn new skills and techniques rapidly. Employers look for this potential, and for the motivation to keep skills up to date. Workers must be able to adapt to change as this is a key feature of the industry.

Client focus

Clients are all-important – the industry revolves around meeting their needs. Workers need to have the client foremost in their minds at all times. This focus should always drive the approach to the project.

Communication skills

Electronic media is all about effective communication. Good communication skills are essential for everyone in the industry, at every level.

Commercial focus

Electronic media is centred around the fast-paced world of business. Maintaining a competitive edge is vital to both the clients of electronic media services and the providers themselves. Awareness of commercial, financial and legal issues is very important to anyone working in this area, especially as many of the companies are small and business environments are always changing.

IT orientation

IT is the central element of electronic media. An interest in IT, and an awareness of developments, is very important to everyone in the industry, regardless of how technical their role is. IT developments create the potential to explore horizons and experiment with new creative forms. Most jobs require competence in particular software and hardware, but the potential to learn and adapt quickly to new developments is more important.

MYTH BUSTER

You need to be a computer boffin to work in electronic media

Technical competence is very important, but many jobs in electronic media also require creative flair. Most of the technology is relatively straightforward to master with a little perseverance – creativity is much harder to learn.

VITAL STATISTICS

A 1997 Skillset survey of people working in broadcasting, film, video and multimedia showed some interesting changes in the industries. In 1989, six out of ten people employed in production, post-production and technical functions were permanent employees. The situation is now reversed, with six out of ten (and rising) now working freelance. The following findings were also made:

- three out of five workers were male, although gender distribution varied through different industry areas
- 66% of freelances were based in the south east of England
- most workers were in the 16–34 age group
- terrestrial TV broadcasting was the largest employment area.

Freelance income levels were as follows in 1998:

Income level	Percentage
Less than £5,999	9%
£6,000–£11,999	10%
£12,000–£19,999	17%
£20,000–£29,999	24%
£30,000–£39,999	16%
£40,000 or more	24%

Source: Skillset Freelance Employment and Training Needs 1998

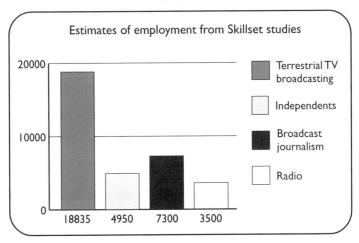

Source: Skillset occupational map 1997

A 1998 survey of National Union of Journalists (NUJ) members found that the majority (around 67%) were on permanent contracts. Around 27% were freelance and around 6% were on short-term contracts.

- Almost half the sample worked wholly or partly in the newspaper sector, split almost evenly between national and provincial newspapers.
- Nearly a third worked in television and radio.
- 61% were male and 39% were female.
- One third was under 35; 59% were 35–54; 10.5% were over 55; 2.2% were under 25.

Location was a significant factor in earning levels. The majority earned £15,000–£24,999, although more than two in five in the Greater London area earned £30,000 or above. The most common job skills (as all or part of the member's work) were editorial:

- editor (28.1%)
- sub-editor (28.5%)
- writer (38.9%)
- reporter (45.3%).

Others skills were:

- photographer (12.8%)
- researcher (13.5%)
- producer (15%).

Source: NUJ Survey Results 1998

Media salaries

Earnings in media jobs can vary considerably depending on the exact nature of the position and your level of experience. Below are typical salary ranges for the jobs outlined earlier in this section. These figures are based on permanent or contract staff at the end of 1999.

Presenter Salaries vary. Local TV and radio presenters may be on quite a low salary. Well-known presenters can command huge fees because they draw audiences.

Broadcast journalist £15,000–£19,000 is a typical starting salary. Salaries above this vary considerably.

Producer £18,000–£20,000 is a typical starting salary. Experienced producers earn anywhere up to £80,000.

Director Extremely variable. Experienced directors can earn anywhere up to £80,000.

Researcher £12,000–£18,000 would be a typical starting salary.

Editor £15,000–£20,000 is a typical starting salary. Experienced editors can earn anything up to £70,000.

Camera operator A starting salary could be between £12,000–£20,000. Experienced camera operators typically earn up to £40,000.

Vision mixer £12,000–£16,000 is a typical starting salary. Experienced vision mixers typically earn £20,000–£30,000.

Production assistant £12,000 would be a typical starting salary. An experienced production assistant (PA) could earn £20,000 or more.

Runner £5,200–£10,000 is common, although many work for free.

Media sales executive For both broadcasting and print, this is usually a combination of basic salary and commission. A typical basic salary would be £12,000–£16,000 or more. Earnings potential is high for people with good selling skills.

Reporter £11,000–£12,000 is a typical starting salary. Experienced reporters could be on £25,000 or more. Salaries are generally higher on national papers.

Features writer £12,000 would be typical for a junior position. Experienced writers typically earn £20,000–£35,000.

Sub-editor £12,000–£15,000 is a typical starting salary. Experienced subs can earn £20,000–£45,000.

Picture researcher £10,000–£12,000 is a typical starting salary. An experienced picture researcher may earn up to £30,000.

Press photographer/photojournalist A starting salary can be anywhere from £10,000–£20,000. Established press photographers can earn £20,000–£50,000. National papers offer the highest salaries.

Graphic designer £10,000–£12,000 is a typical starting salary. Experienced graphic designers can earn £18,000–£30,000.

In the first part of this *Insider Career Guide* we have taken an overview of the media industries. In Part Two, we go on to look at the people who work in them and how you can evaluate your skills in order to make career decisions.

part two   the person

the person

> 'The difference between a successful person and others is not a
> lack of strength, not a lack of knowledge, but rather a lack of will.'
> *Vincent T. Lombardi (1913–1970), US football coach*

Introduction

In Part One, we took a broad view of the media industries
and looked at some important job areas within them. Part
Two is about people, and you in particular. We will look at
the requirements of employers, education and training, how
to decide what you want to do, and how to assess your skills,
strengths and weaknesses.

WHAT DO EMPLOYERS WANT?

Although different jobs require particular skills and personal
characteristics, there are some attributes sought by virtually
all employers. There are three skill areas that are required
for almost every job in any industry:

- **Transferable skills** Roles are subject to change in
  many industries and this is particularly true of the
  media. Employers look for generic skills that can be
  applied in a wide range of situations.
- **Communication skills** Few jobs exist in isolation,
  so the ability to communicate well, both verbally
  and in writing, is vital. The media are particularly
  geared towards people working in teams.
- **Organising skills** All employers want staff who can
  manage their work effectively as this impacts directly
  on business. This is a key requirement for any media job
  and a necessity for freelances.

There are further characteristics that most employers will be on the lookout for:

- cheerful and helpful personality
- smart appearance
- initiative
- self-motivation
- enthusiasm and keenness
- responsibility and reliability
- adaptability
- people skills – able to get on with colleagues, customers, etc.
- understanding of the role and the organisation
- ability to work without supervision.

Media skills

The acronym ACE spells out the three essential attributes all media employers look for:

- **Aptitude** Where you are now is less important than where you have the capability to go. Specific skills, especially relating to technology, can become redundant very quickly in the media. Employers want people who can develop and continually expand their skills to meet changing requirements.
- **Commitment** Working in the media is often a lifestyle choice rather than a job. Employers look for dedication and passion. A demonstrable interest and involvement in the media before graduating from college or applying for your first job will help convince employers of your suitability.
- **Experience** It's hard to get even the lowest level media job without some relevant experience. Unpaid experience may be a necessity and helps prove your commitment and initiative.

Research by Skillset, the national media training organisation, has identified further abilities required for almost any job.

The most important skill:

- the ability to establish and maintain good working relationships, and to work safely.

Other requirements:

- creative skills
- computer literacy
- business/financial awareness
- the ability to work under pressure
- the ability to meet deadlines
- a flexible/problem-solving approach.

New horizons, new skills

Take a look back at the section on electronic media skills. All areas of broadcasting and media are becoming more commercially focused and high-tech, and work is increasingly team and project based. The skills outlined in that section can be applied across the board.

New developments in the media industry, particularly the convergence of the media, IT and telecommunications industries, mean a demand for new skills. Employers are increasingly looking for people with skills and training in aspects of IT and telecommunications as well as the more traditional media skills. Remember that being employable in the media is all about adapting to what the market needs.

'We look for passion and commitment – these are the most important ingredients for broadcasting personnel. There are plenty of wannabes, but those with real dedication are worth their weight in gold.'

HR manager

MYTH BUSTER
Media is an industry for 'arty' types

Creativity is very important in all areas of the media, but technology is a dominant force in the industry. People with strong scientific and technical ability are highly valued.

WHAT DO YOU WANT?

Finding the ideal job is not easy. This is a fact we all have to face. Among your friends and acquaintances there will probably be a good number who are dissatisfied with their work for one reason or another.

Perhaps they don't have the scope for creativity they want, or their skills are not being put to good use. Maybe they want more responsibility, or feel at sea in a large anonymous organisation, or dislike having to deal with the public. It could just be they are not paid enough.

Many people enter jobs that don't really suit their skills or temperament. They feel unfulfilled. And there is another side to this; hundreds of people apply for jobs for which they don't have the necessary skills, aptitude or personality. They are rejected, probably without even getting an interview. It is likely that many of you reading this book have experienced this. So can this unhappy state of affairs be avoided?

The answer is yes – at least to a certain extent. Making the right choice involves taking a thorough look at yourself. This may seem obvious, and you may think you know yourself well, but self-assessment does need to be approached in a structured way. It's all too easy to overlook personal attributes, skills, experience and preferences that could be important in deciding on a career path. You need to be methodical and ruthlessly honest in examining your aptitudes and preferences in relation to jobs. What you discover about yourself can be surprising.

ABOUT YOU

Self-assessment is the key to targeting jobs suitable for you. It must be stressed that this only works *if you have researched the job carefully.* (We will look at this in more detail a little further on). If you don't have a realistic idea of what a job involves, how can you decide if it's right for you?

There are a number of professionally developed self-assessment tools available, some of which may well be useful, particularly if you are uncertain about what you want to do. These are available through your local careers office, and some can even be found on the Internet. It is a good idea, however, to start with a bit of investigation of your own. The important points to think about are your:

- personality
- interests, preferences and dislikes
- skills and achievements
- strengths and weaknesses.

This section gives a few informal self-assessment activities. These are not scored in any way – they are just intended to get you thinking about yourself and your choices. Activities like these can point you to job areas you hadn't considered, or help you decide if a job you're thinking about is really for you.

Career choice

There are a lot of different factors involved in choosing a career, including pay, geographical location and availability of work. Remember there are many more reasons than just money for having a job. Everyone gains something different from work. Consider the following examples:

- social interaction
- a sense of identity
- enhancing existing skills and developing new ones
- the opportunity to make a contribution
- a sense of purpose and direction.

On a long-term basis, a career is only likely to be satisfying if it matches your skills, interests and personality.

Your interests

Think carefully about these. What gives you satisfaction?

- Try to think of both general and specific activities, and *make a list.*

This is important – writing things down gives your mind something to focus on and helps you to organise your thoughts. Examples might include:

- technical work
- managing people
- working with your hands
- using figures
- using computers.

Think of as many examples as you can.

- Once you have made your list, pick out the interests that are most important to you and list them in order of priority.

Would these be important features of a job? Do they figure in jobs you may be considering?

Your dislikes

Dislikes are as important as interests. What don't you like doing?

- Make a list of things you would definitely prefer not to be a major aspect of your job.

Include aspects of your present job or any other work you have done. Are any of these things likely to feature in jobs you are considering?

The balancing act

Any job will usually involve a certain amount of compromise. You have to balance the aspects you may not be so keen on against the positive factors. Few people find jobs that are absolutely perfect, but an acceptable balance is possible – the positive should outweigh the negative. Try to weigh up your likes and dislikes. Which are the most important factors? Would a compromise be workable?

Your skills

You gain skills in a variety of ways, not just through work. Leisure activities, education and experience, such as bringing up a family, can all provide you with skills that are valuable to an employer.

- Now start making a list of all the skills you have acquired, in as many contexts as you can think of.

It is very useful to group your skills under headings. The following examples may serve as a guideline. Try to come up with your own additional headings. Some skills will fall into more than one category. Think of both general and specific skills. And be honest – list only those skills that you actually possess.

Communication skills
- making presentations
- putting ideas across to colleagues, potential investors, etc.
- dealing with customers/the public
- report writing.

Creative skills
- designing/drawing
- directing
- writing and editing
- coming up with ideas/solutions.

Organisation and planning
- prioritising work effectively
- developing aims and objectives
- anticipating future needs
- admin skills.

Teamworking/people skills
- working effectively on group projects
- understanding team dynamics and roles
- sensitivity to colleagues' needs
- recognising contribution of others.

Problem-solving
- lateral thinking
- prioritising problems
- holistic view – understanding the context in which a problem occurs
- troubleshooting and developing strategies.

Technical aptitude
- computer literacy
- experience of software packages
- knowledge of sound/lighting techniques
- electronics/engineering.

Management skills
- leading and motivating a team
- making decisions
- having responsibility
- strategic planning.

Financial management
- administering a budget
- balancing accounts
- negotiating contracts
- market knowledge.

Research the job

If there is a job or career area you are interested in, you need to do some detailed research. Here are some of the questions you should be asking:

- What skills are required?
- What experience is expected?
- What personality characteristics are desirable?

- What are the duties and responsibilities?
- What is the salary range?
- What are the prospects for promotion/career development?
- Who will I be working with?
- What are the working conditions like?
- What is the industry culture like?

Finding the answers to questions such as these will help you identify your most relevant skills and match your experience with the job's requirements.

Strengths and weaknesses

Now that you have taken an in-depth look at your skills and the requirements of the career area you're interested in, you should have a good idea of where your strengths lie. You will probably also have recognised some weaknesses – perhaps areas where you lack skills and experience. It is as important to identify weaknesses as it is to identify strengths. These are usually not insurmountable problems, but they are issues you need to address to make yourself employable.

- Write a list of weaknesses you have identified.
- Make an action plan for each one – how will you get the knowledge/skill, etc. that you need?

This is an extremely useful exercise. Remember that most employers are looking for aptitude. They won't necessarily expect you to have all the desired skills, but they will want to see that you are aware of any lack of experience and know how to address it. Everyone working in the media must be able to identify their skills update needs.

You can try some more formal self-assessments on the Internet at the following sites:

www1.kaplan.com/view/article/0,1898,1411,00.html

www.bgsu.edu/offices/careers/process/step1.html

www.careerlab.com/art_likes.htm

www2.ncsu.edu/unity/lockers/users/l/lkj/

'You can't know if something's right for you until you've tried it. I was desperate to be a cameraman. After doing some workshops I decided it just wasn't where I wanted to go.'

Journalist

Case Study
Chief graphic artist

I began doing a degree in fine art, but realised this was not the course for me and switched to art history. On graduating, I wasn't exactly sure what I wanted to do. I thought illustration might be the direction I wanted to go in so I started putting a portfolio of work together. I tried to include quite a variety of styles – photo montages, line drawings, cartoons, paintings, etc.

I spoke to a company that was looking for someone to do freelance illustration. Although this didn't happen, they put me in touch with the head of the graphics department at the local paper. They had a vacancy for a junior graphic artist. Initially, I had an informal meeting with the head of department. I was concerned that not having a graphics degree would be an obstacle, but this did not turn out to be the case. The job was fairly low paid and they were prepared to give training. After a second, more formal, interview I was offered the job. I had put a lot of effort into my portfolio and this was probably what got me in. I had to work a three-month probationary period before being offered a permanent contract.

On-the-job training was pretty good – the paper sent me on a variety of training courses, one of which was in Germany. After three years, the head of department left. By this time, I had enough experience and confidence to apply for the job. I was successful and have been in my present job for two years. Because it's a small department, we pretty much do the same work – there isn't a really obvious hierarchy.

An important part of our work is information graphics. These are graphic illustrations that give information that can't be easily put across in words. In the case of a major train crash, we might do a graphic showing the sequence of events, perhaps with cutaway diagrams, etc. and relevant technical information. We do a variety of other graphics including charts and graphs for business features, topical caricatures and small illustrations to go in features. Some are produced on computer, others are hand-drawn. We also do front cover design for magazines and supplements.

There is some crossover with the work of the sub-editors. We work quite closely with them and agree between us who will do what. Liaison with other departments is an important part of the job – we keep close contact with the journalists, who supply us with the breaking news stories, and with the picture desk to ensure there aren't any conflicting pictures or repeats.

This is a very enjoyable job on the whole and we have quite a lot of creative freedom. The main frustrations are caused by time pressures – deadlines are always looming. Sometimes I'm not happy with a graphic or illustration because I haven't had time to complete it as I would like, but that's just the nature of working in newspapers.

EDUCATION AND TRAINING

Qualifications are still an important factor in getting a job in the media, and in moving up the career ladder. This section considers a few important points you should take into account when making your educational decisions.

What about A levels?

Your choice of A level subjects depends largely on the work you're interested in and the requirements of any higher education courses you may be considering. If it's technical work that grabs you, science subjects and maths are useful. English is a valuable subject if you have any kind of journalistic leanings. Don't overlook art if you want a creative/design role. Computer science would be relevant to virtually any job these days.

A question of degree

Should I do a degree or try to get straight into work? This is a question asked by many people considering media careers. Unfortunately there is no completely straightforward answer to this. The decision you make depends on a number of factors, such as:

- the job you want
- your financial situation
- your education and training history
- your work experience and current situation.

Some jobs, such as journalism, are very hard to get into without a degree and postgraduate qualifications. You will be up against a lot of competition for any job you apply for. Much of the competition will be graduates – many of them media graduates – all as keen as you to get the job. A degree may not be a requirement but you will certainly have to outshine the competition and prove why it is *you* and not *them* that should be employed.

A degree can give you:

- transferable skills, such as researching and time management
- a chance to assess what you really want to do while gaining a valuable qualification
- practical training relevant to a job
- opportunities to network with peers and employers
- better prospects for promotion.

There is more to doing a degree than just acquiring skills and knowledge. Being a student can be an unforgettable and character-shaping experience. Many people are happier during their student days than at any other time in their lives. The social side is a big part of this. Another factor is the access to facilities and equipment – anyone interested in media will have the opportunity to develop relevant skills.

Should I do media studies?

This question sparks a lot of controversy. Media studies courses have been criticised for failing to provide practical training relevant to the industry, being too theoretical and academic, and churning out graduates who can deconstruct the sub-text of *Coronation Street* but can't operate even the most basic equipment.

This kind of criticism is perhaps a bit extreme but not without foundation. Many media courses provide very good training in the practical aspects of the business and have established links with employers. Some employ staff who are currently working in media and therefore have their finger on the industry's pulse. A few are funded and run in conjunction with broadcasters such as the BBC. There are a huge number of media courses being run across the country. It is inevitable that some will be good, some not so good. Finding the right one for you is important.

A media degree is no guarantee that you will be able to get a media job. There are currently more students on relevant media studies courses than there are employees in the whole of the BBC. There are simply not enough jobs to go around. However, if you want to get some hands-on experience and, perhaps, try out some different media roles before deciding on the career you want, a media course could be for you.

Passing a degree shows that you can work independently, are able to absorb complex information, communicate ideas and concentrate over a period of time. You are also likely to have acquired research, analysis and learning skills. All these factors are important to media employers. However, these important skills relate to any degree. Channel 4's head of personnel once commented: '...we want discipline and intellect. You are as likely to get a job with a science degree as with one in media studies.'

The most important point is to think carefully about what you want to study. Don't do media just because you think you might want a job in it. Consider what subjects you have a really strong interest in – you're more likely to do well at these. And doing a subject other than media doesn't mean you can't get into the industry.

If you decide that a media course is what you need, it is essential to find the right one for you. Consider the skills you want to get and the sort of work you want to do before selecting a course. There are a number of important factors to look out for when deciding on a course. Do your research carefully. If possible, speak to current and former students and find out about the following:

- **Accreditation** Make sure the qualification you get will be recognised by employers and relevant professional bodies. Industry training organisations (such as Skillset and the NCTJ) have lists of accredited courses that have been approved for content and relevance.

- **Facilities** Levels of equipment and facilities vary so make sure you will have access to the technology you want to gain skills in.
- **Industry links** Does the establishment have established contacts with employers so you will be able to get relevant work experience? This could be important in making contacts for future employment.
- **Staff** Do the staff have experience as industry professionals?
- **Course content** Is the focus on practical or theoretical aspects? Will it teach you what you want to learn?

Postgraduate qualifications

One thing about the media is that you are unlikely to be deemed overqualified for any job you might go for. Even if postgraduate qualifications are not a requirement, they certainly won't do you any harm. Having a higher qualification in any subject shows you have research and independent working skills.

A postgraduate journalism qualification is particularly useful. Journalism gives you a lot of skills that are very relevant to many areas of broadcasting and the media. Starting your media career as a journalist can be an advantage – you won't be starting at the very bottom of the ladder and there are many directions you could branch off into.

Other media skills courses

If you flick through the media recruitment section of one of the national newspapers you will see a host of advertisements for courses purporting to train you as a journalist, editor, radio presenter, etc. Some of these are correspondence courses, others are short-duration intensive courses, some take place over a series of weekends. All will relieve you of your hard-earned money. That is not to say these courses have no worth. Some are probably very good. However, some are undoubtedly not. Be wary of any course promising you an easy ticket into media work – it simply doesn't work like that.

The same advice goes for choosing a media degree. Investigate carefully what the course can actually offer, and whether the qualification is worth the paper it is printed on to an employer. Weigh up the cost of the course against what you will actually gain before you commit yourself. Arrange to speak to people who have done the course – a college worth its salt should be happy to help with this. If you want to be sure you're not throwing your money away, choose a course accredited by a professional body such as Skillset or the NCTJ.

'Qualifications are still important. A degree shows you can apply yourself and be disciplined – the subject isn't too important. You may have all the talent in the world, but if you don't have any qualifications employers will wonder why.'

Recruitment consultant

Case Study
Freelance camera operator/editor

My interest in broadcasting started even before I went to university. I did a Community Services Volunteers (CSV) placement where I worked as an assistant to two disabled TV producers. Initially I was just helping to carry equipment, driving the van and generally helping out. I started to develop an interest in what they were doing and began assisting with the editing process. I was just doing fairly routine stuff but I found it very exciting. This gave me the initial idea that I might eventually like to work in television.

Shortly after my placement I went to university to study physics. This scientific background has proved quite helpful in my broadcasting career. While at university, I joined the TV society. We attempted to make programmes and I got my first real hands-on experience. This actually turned out to be very useful and was almost certainly a factor in me getting my first job.

After graduation, I saw an advert in the media section of *The Guardian* for trainee recording operators with the BBC. This was a fairly low-level position in the video editing department.

I applied, had two interviews and eventually received a letter offering me a job at the BBC.

I spent four years working for the BBC in London. I quickly progressed to assistant editor, and eventually to editor. After this time, I decided I wanted to leave London and moved up north where I worked for BBC regional companies. I was doing editing and an increasing amount of camera work. I did this for some two years, eventually finding that local news was not interesting enough – there are only so many ways you can try to make local council features exciting!

Going freelance seemed the best move as I wanted more variety. The contacts I had were essential. Initially, I freelanced mainly for the BBC companies I had been working for. Without good contacts, and a good reputation for quality work behind me, I would have struggled to get by. It's a decision I'm glad I made – the greater variety of work keeps me motivated and I have more freedom. I currently only choose to work an average of three days a week. Quality of life and having time for other interests is important. The downside is probably the amount of time I can spend on motorways, travelling up and down the country. This is a feature of the job.

I now do a combination of camera work and editing. I find the work satisfying and enjoy the creative aspects, such as coming up with new ideas and composing shots artistically. It's a great feeling when something works well. I work mainly on news programmes, features, documentaries and magazine programmes. These kinds of programmes are great to work on, although I would like to do some longer and more high-profile documentaries.

These days, I am more into the camera side of things, but being able to edit as well makes me more marketable. Having more than one skill is a bonus. As a freelance you rely on your skills to keep you in work. It's important to keep them up-to-date. This can be difficult – finding the time is the main problem. I am shortly going to start an NVQ course. These are beginning to be recognised and looked for by employers, so it could well be useful to have this official recognition of my skills.

IS MEDIA THE RIGHT CAREER FOR ME?

In the last section, we looked at ways to assess your skills and aptitudes and weigh up the suitability of jobs or areas of work. In this section, we will take a look at some important trends in the media industry culture which you need to take into account when considering what you might like to do. Think about how these match your skills, preferences and personality.

Freelancing

How do you feel about working freelance? Freelance work is becoming increasingly common in all areas of the media. In some, it has become the norm – it is becoming much harder to find permanent employment in the media. Whereas going freelance is often a choice for established professionals, people now entering some areas of the industry will find they can only get work on a freelance basis.

There are pros and cons to this way of working. Freelancing can offer:

- a greater variety of work
- more control over your working life
- the chance to work for different companies
- freedom to plan your own time
- less routine
- higher rates of pay.

But there is a downside:

- lack of security
- no sick pay, holiday pay, pension, etc.
- having to be always on the lookout for work
- responsibility for your own tax, national insurance, etc.
- no stable, familiar work environment
- unpredictable financial ups and downs.

'The great thing about this kind of work is the freedom and control it gives you. You can plan your work around the rest of your life and you are not under anyone's control. I don't think I would consider going back to permanent employment. The downside of freelancing is, perhaps, the lack of career structure. You are jumping from job to job all the time, so you don't get a definite progression as you might working for an employer where there is often a defined promotion route. It's fairly easy to make a living, but harder to build a career. Another aspect is that you may miss the social aspect of work if you are working from home most of the time.'

Freelance features writer

Freelances need a variety of skills and aptitudes in addition to the specific requirements of their actual work. For example:

- **Business acumen** As a freelance, you are running your own business and, therefore, need some skill in areas such as managing your accounts and tax, financial planning and pricing of your services.

- **Self-marketing** If you are blessed with great skill and luck, work will just come to you. Most freelances, however, need to know how to market themselves effectively. This is especially true if you are just starting out and don't have an established reputation or portfolio behind you.

- **Work planning** As a freelance you could be doing work for a variety of different companies. You need good planning skills to ensure that your time is used effectively and you are available at the most crucial times for each company.

- **Market awareness** Freelances are only in demand if they have skills and knowledge that people need. Keeping your finger on the pulse is vital. You will have to keep on top of changing skills needs.

- **Self-motivation** Because you are totally in charge of your career and working patterns, you need to be very self-motivated. You won't have a manager to help you progress in your career. Also, you will have to maintain your energy and enthusiasm to keep things moving and to get yourself through any difficult patches.

- **Professionalism** A freelance has to be thoroughly professional, probably even more so than an employee. This includes both your actual work and your general approach and attitude. You are providing a professional service – if you are less than reliable you won't be asked back.

'Being tolerant, controlled and friendly is essential for a freelance. If you annoy people they won't want to use you again, it's as simple as that. Being conscientious and dedicated will get you a long way. You have to have the attitude that you will always do the best job you can, even if you think people are not appreciating you fully. In the course of my editing work I sometimes come across other camera people's rushes which show no evidence of imagination or effort, as if they're just going through the motions. Making that extra effort is what distinguishes a true professional.'

Freelance camera operator

Short-term contracts

Fixed-term contracts are also increasingly common. It is quite usual for an employer to offer a six-month contract, even for ongoing work.

This is perhaps the least attractive feature of media work. However, people are prepared to put up with the fact that even long-term jobs can have little security because the work is so interesting. Lots of people want to be in the industry, so even low-paid and insecure jobs are much sought after. Think carefully if security is one of your top priorities.

One thing you can say about this system is that it rewards merit. There is less 'dead wood' than in other industries because people without skills and talent simply don't make it.

'The business studies course I did has proved very useful. TV work revolves around short-term contracts. The reality is that you may well have to find other work to fill in the gaps between these contracts. Skills and qualifications in other areas of work can come in very handy.'

TV researcher

Youth culture

All the media are tending towards an increasingly young workforce. The majority of workers in most areas are in the 16–34 age group. It can be difficult to make a career change into media later in life, unless you have a lot of relevant experience. The convergence with newer industries such as multimedia and Internet technologies is likely to create more jobs for people at the younger end of the spectrum.

The fast pace of change

The fast-developing technology and rapid pace of change in the industry have been mentioned numerous times in this book. This is an important feature of the industry and cannot be overstated. It is another factor in the increasing youth of the workforce – a dynamic and rapidly changing environment is exciting to younger people but can lose its appeal as you grow older.

Small companies

The media industry is characterised by an increasing number of small companies. This is largely due to the low-cost and easy-to-use new technology. The trend applies to all areas, from radio and TV production and post-production companies to magazines and newsletters. A company's workforce may be as small as two or three people, expanded with freelances as and when necessary. There are, of course, a lot of larger employers, but numbers remain fairly static.

Graduate professions

It is becoming harder to get into any media job without a degree or relevant professional qualifications. Journalism is becoming almost exclusively a graduate profession. Graduates may be sought even for entry-level positions, such as TV studio runner.

JUST FOR FUN...

Freelancing quiz

Think freelancing may be for you? Try this short quiz. It's a bit of fun and obviously not intended as a definitive assessment of your suitability. Still, it may help you focus on how freelancing would fit with your personal characteristics.

1. When your bank statement arrives, are the credits and debits...

    a. expected and planned for
    b. a source of mystery and wonder
    c. neither of the above because it goes in the bin unopened?

2. If you have several tasks to complete in a day, do you...
    a. ascertain the order of importance and judge how long each will take before starting
    b. do the ones that look the most fun first
    c. leave them all until tomorrow – you might feel more like it then?

3. If you have to work irregular hours, do you...
    a. enjoy the change and variety
    b. grumble a bit but do it anyway
    c. refuse – anything other than nine to five is unacceptable?

4. Filling in a tax return would be:
    a. no problem with adequate planning and preparation
    b. a real nuisance
    c. only marginally preferable to swimming with piranhas.

5. If you have an important piece of work to complete by a certain date, do you...
    a. arrange your work and social life to ensure you have enough time
    b. make a reasonable effort but expect the deadline can be extended
    c. let them wait – it can't be as important as your darts practice?

6. Working from home would be:
    a. great, because not having to commute gives you more working time
    b. OK, but there'd be a lot of distractions
    c. a good excuse to watch TV and play computer games.

7. Dividing your week between several different workplaces would be:
    a. stimulating and challenging
    b. a bit of a drag
    c. impossible – it's hard enough keeping track of what you're supposed to be doing when you're only in one place.

8. Having the freedom to plan your daily activities is:
    a. very important as you know how you work best
    b. quite nice sometimes, but it means you have to think a lot
    c. scary – you'd rather be told what to do.

9. If you didn't have a manager overseeing you, would you...
    a. enjoy using your own initiative and talent to progress your career
    b. be unsure what to do next
    c. work less and play more golf?

10. The most important aspect of work is:
    a. variety and being in control
    b. the money
    c. a staff canteen with good chips and a subsidised bar.

If you answered mostly (a), you should have no problem coping with freelancing. If you answered mainly (b) or (c), you should think carefully about whether freelancing is for you.

Are you a media fanatic?

Are you obsessed with the media? Do new developments fascinate and enthral you? Test your media general knowledge with this quiz. Check your answers at the end of the quiz.

1. A grip is:
    a. a TV broadcasting technician who sets up equipment
    b. a video editor
    c. something you lose under pressure.

2. Hyperlinks are:
    a. useful media contacts
    b. high-speed computer networks
    c. tags in an electronic document that take you to another page or location.

3. Pixels are:
    a. picture cells – the dots making up a TV or printed picture
    b. online picture libraries
    c. old-fashioned radio transmitters.

4. Reuters is:
    a. a stress-related illness common in media personnel
    b. a news agency
    c. a digital broadcasting company.

5. A syndicate is:
    a. the management team of a radio station
    b. an independent TV station
    c. a combined group of newspapers.

6. Avid is:
    a. a software application for video editing
    b. a new type of lightweight TV camera
    c. the necessary attitude for broadcasting staff.

7. Linear editing is:
    a. a less creative style of editing used in serious documentaries
    b. a factory production line approach used by large corporations
    c. real-time editing for film.

8. Post-production is:
    a. the process of making TV programmes interactive
    b. the process of editing, etc. that takes place after footage has been shot
    c. a new technique for delivering news by e-mail.

9. Wowing is:
    a. using shock tactics to impress an audience
    b. a temporary loss of sound during broadcasting
    c. the sound produced when a DJ starts a record before the turntable has reached full speed.

10. Java is:
    a. the country with the largest newspaper readership in the world
    b. an Internet programming language
    c. the preferred caffeine source of most reporters.

And the answers are...
1a; 2c; 3a; 4b; 5c; 6a; 7c; 8b; 9c; 10b.

If you got less than five right, you may need to do some further research into the media. Good background knowledge is very helpful in landing a job.

Case Study
Freelance presenter and journalist

My broadcasting career really started at the age of 14 when I got involved in hospital radio. I was obsessed with radio and never wanted to do anything else. At this tender age, I ended up having my own hour-long show on Sunday evenings! At 17, I started doing voluntary work for a local BBC radio station. I answered the phones and generally helped out. After a time, they started letting me do the odd interview and research for programmes.

I knew a broadcasting career was what I wanted and went to university to do communications and cultural studies. My holidays were spent volunteering back at the radio station. I got some of my most valuable experience in this way. After my degree, I did a postgraduate diploma in broadcast journalism. I then went back to a full-time job as a news reporter with the radio station. I got interested in producing and eventually ended up as the producer on the breakfast show.

My next career change occurred because I was interested in doing some TV work. I started freelancing as a bi-media producer, doing a bit of radio and a bit of TV. An important part of that was adapting stuff the TV reporters had done into a form suitable for radio. With this experience under my belt, I managed to get a job with one of the ITV companies as a newsreader on a regional news programme. After about a year, I felt I wanted to work in radio again. I spent a year at Classic FM as a newsreader then moved back to the BBC as a producer at the world service.

I now work freelance, doing a mixture of voiceover work, continuity announcing for TV and radio journalism/feature making. The voiceover work is mainly a mixture of radio adverts and informational material, such as audio versions of government leaflets for the visually impaired. Continuity announcers make the links between programmes, hopefully ensuring a smooth transition. You have to monitor the outgoing and incoming programmes, check you can join the next broadcast and make sure your link fits the amount of time specified for it. The other aspect of my work is radio journalism – reporting and making features. This involves interviewing, assembling footage and sound effects, writing scripts, then pulling everything together into something cohesive that can be broadcast.

I like the freedom that freelance work gives me. Voice work, such as announcing, is enjoyable but I now prefer to do prerecorded rather than live work – it's much less stressful.

To succeed in broadcasting you've got to really want to do it – you need a bit of an obsession with media. A good idea of what you want to do will help you to fix goals. The most important thing is to just start doing it – putting yourself out there and getting the experience however you can. You need to be flexible and prepared to do everything – even the mundane and less pleasant tasks.

There are more and more radio stations and TV channels so there is work out there – they all need presenters, announcers, producers, etc. In commercial radio and TV, a lot of what is being done is repackaging of old material and old programmes. Even the new programmes often just follow a format that is tried and tested and therefore 'safe'. At the moment there is less work on programming of an experimental or slightly daring nature.

In Part Two of this book we have looked at the skills requirements for the media industries and at how to effectively analyse your own skills. In Part Three, we examine the process of finding and applying for jobs and how to present yourself in the best possible light.

part three

getting in, getting on... getting out

getting in, getting on... getting out

> 'Nothing in this world can take the place of persistence... Persistence and determination alone are omnipotent. The slogan "press on" has solved and always will solve the problems of the human race.'
>
> *Calvin Coolidge (1872–1933), 30th US President*

Introduction

This third part of the book gives you the low-down on the process of getting into the media industry and on your options for progressing or moving into other industries.

Having read the first two parts of the book, you should have a fairly good idea of how competitive media is. To get in, you have to present yourself as the outstanding candidate and outshine the competition. To get on you have to demonstrate your competence, professionalism and willingness to learn and adapt.

In the last section, we looked at the skills employers require and asked you to think about your own skills and how they fit in with jobs. Now we go a step further and apply this knowledge to the procedures you will go through in order to get a job.

GETTING IN

To get a job you must know how to look for appropriate openings and how to successfully negotiate the recruitment procedure. There are a number of possible stages to the process, each requiring some specific skills:

- finding the vacancies
- creating a portfolio of work

- writing CVs and covering letters
- completing application forms
- attending interviews
- attending assessment centres
- making presentations
- taking psychometric tests.

Candidates are weeded out at every stage so it is important to pay equal care and attention to each one.

Finding the vacancies

There are a number of ways to go about finding openings. Be prepared to try all of them. The more time and effort you put in, the greater your chances of success.

- **The press** Media jobs are advertised in national and local papers, as well as trade and specialist publications (see *Want to read all about it?*). There are a growing number of national and regional recruitment publications that have sections for media vacancies.
- **The direct method** Many jobs are never advertised. Writing speculative letters to employers can be a good way to find work. If you happen to write just when they are looking for someone with your skills you might get lucky. Employers will often keep your CV on file in case your skills match upcoming jobs.
- **The Internet** If you surf the net you will discover a wealth of sites devoted to recruitment, some of which specialise in media jobs. See *Want to find out more?* for some suggestions.
- **Agencies** There are a variety of specialist media recruitment agencies all over the country which can help you find work on a permanent, temporary or freelance basis. It is worth registering with a few.
- **Contacts** Making and maintaining contacts is an invaluable way to get on in the media. A great deal of work is allocated through personal recommendation, again bypassing the recruitment process.

> Given the choice, an employer will always go for someone whose abilities they know.

The process of finding a job can seem intimidating. You will find it easier and feel more in control if you approach the process in a structured and methodical way. The following ideas are tried and tested.

- **Time management** Use your time well. Set aside time, every day if possible, for your job search activities. Create a schedule and try to do regular tasks at the same time each day. Use a diary to plan your activities.
- **Keeping track** It's all too easy to lose track of what you have applied for and when. Keeping a log is very useful and will enable you to follow up at the right time. Record formal and speculative applications, and any informal contacts you make that might need following up. Note who you have spoken or written to, the dates of any correspondence and any action you need to take. Keep all job-related paperwork in a file.
- **Setting targets** Job-hunting can seem very unrewarding at times and it is easy to lose motivation. Setting yourself targets – daily and longer-term – is a big help in retaining your sense of purpose and achievement. You can set targets for any activity, including letter writing, sending out CVs and making phone calls. Only set targets you can realistically achieve.

Creating a good portfolio of work

A good portfolio is essential for getting any media job. Your portfolio is an indication of your experience and shows employers what you are capable of. What you put in depends on the type of work you are trying to get, but it should be as comprehensive as possible. You can include examples of work and other useful information, such as:

- published or unpublished articles/pieces you have written

- video/audio tapes
- details of projects you have worked on
- showreels
- references from employers or organisations you have worked for.

And it doesn't have to be just things you've done in a work situation – even your spare time activities can be valuable evidence of your capabilities.

A showreel is usually a video or audio tape that showcases you and your work. This could be recordings of yourself presenting mock TV or radio shows, or some footage you have edited or produced. It will indicate your ability and potential much better than a CV.

It is important for your portfolio to be well-presented as this shows your professionalism. It is worth spending time, and possibly even some money, on getting it as slick as you can. Update your portfolio on a regular basis to reflect your current skills and interests.

The Insider guide to writing effective CVs

Your CV is one of the most important self-marketing tools since it is often the first contact you have with a potential employer. It may be your only chance to convince them you are the right person for the job. This being the case, your CV must make you stand out from the crowd and put across your skills and experience in the best possible light. There are several formats you can use, depending on the job you are going for and the emphasis you want to give. A CV is normally sent with a covering letter.

A CV should contain everything an employer needs to know. It must also be as concise as possible and all the information should be easy to locate. An employer may have to wade through hundreds of CVs. If the relevant details can't be obtained quickly, a CV will probably end up in the bin.

- **How many pages?** The length of your CV is a compromise between being concise and getting all the information across. The balance will depend partly on the seniority of the job you are after. For a higher level job, you will be expected to have a lot of skills and experience, and a longer CV. A two-page CV should cover most situations. Four pages is the absolute maximum.

- **Target it** Your CV needs to be specifically geared to the job in question. You must emphasise the aspects of your skills and experience that make you suitable for that particular job. This means reworking your CV for every job you apply for. You should have a template, or a number of templates, which you can adjust as necessary.

- **Consider the format** This will depend on how you want to portray yourself. Some employers may want you to use a format they specify. The BBC, for example, requests a particular structure – details are available on its website. Some employers may be put off by non-traditional formats.

- **Professional presentation** Keep it clear and simple and avoid gimmicks. Print it on the best quality paper you can get. Never send out photocopies.

The reverse chronological CV is the most popular format. This details your experience in date order, giving the most recent first and working backwards. Responsibilities and achievements are given for each job. The basic structure might be as follows:

- Personal details – name, address, telephone numbers, e-mail address, date of birth.
- Professional qualifications and membership of relevant professional bodies.
- Education and training – you can include exams taken and pending, qualifications and grades.
- Employment history – details of employers, positions held and responsibilities and achievements. Include any voluntary work or work experience.
- Skills – include relevant ones such as IT skills.
- Additional information – anything relevant such as driving licence or first aid training.

- Leisure interests – especially those relevant to the job.
- Employers' references – optional, although some employers may request details of two referees.

Another example is the functional CV. This places the emphasis on skills and achievements rather than job details and can be useful for someone with a patchy work history or a number of jobs that are not obviously relevant experience. Using this format, you would list just the bare details of employers – company, job title and dates – and outline your skills/abilities/ achievements under separate headings. These can be very specific to the job being applied for. Bear in mind that this type of CV may be harder to scan for information.

When writing your CV:

- Collect the information. Gather all the details of your employment, skills, interests, etc. Use the results of the exercises in Part Two of this book.
- Decide what you are going to include. Discard anything that may not be relevant.
- Write your first draft. Think carefully about every word you use – each one must earn its place. Use short sentences or note form and bullet lists rather than big chunks of text.
- Edit the draft – preferably after a bit of time as you will be more objective. Be ruthless. Rewrite until it gives exactly the impact you want. Make sure you eliminate all spelling mistakes and typing errors.
- Get a second opinion. Show it to other people, particularly those with some knowledge of what media employers want. Don't be precious and be prepared to act on advice and criticism.

The Insider guide to writing effective covering letters

It is standard practice to accompany a CV with a covering letter. This should outline the main points of your experience and suitability for the job. As with a CV, it should be concise, relevant and businesslike. The outline should be something like this:

- Addresses – yours in the top right-hand corner, the recipient's name and address in the top left.
- Date.
- Salutation – always try to write to a named person.
- Job title where advertised and date reference if there is one (set all this out in bold on a separate line).
- State why the advert interested you.
- Outline your relevant skills and experience and why you should be considered (you can break up the text with bullet lists).
- Indicate that you look forward to hearing from them.
- Sign off – 'yours sincerely' for a named person, 'yours faithfully' if addressed as Dear Sir/Madam. Sign by hand, with your name typed underneath.
- Avoid too much repetition of the information in your CV or application form.

Some companies may ask you to apply in writing. In this case, your letter should be much more detailed than a covering letter, although the same basic principles apply. The letter should contain all the information the employer needs. You may still want to enclose a copy of your CV for good measure.

You may be asked to apply in your own handwriting. This usually means the organisation is employing a graphologist to assess your character and suitability on the basis of your handwriting. There is not really anything you can do to give a better impression. Write as clearly and legibly as you can but use your natural style.

The Insider guide to completing application forms

CVs tend to be the application method preferred by media employers, but you may still come across some that prefer to use application forms. The advantage of the application form is in comparing large volumes of applications. Details will all be in the same place on the form so the reader can locate them straightaway.

You should normally send a covering letter with an application form, and you may want to include a copy of your CV. Don't rely on this being read – make sure everything relevant is on the application form.

You may think you can't go wrong with an application form, but it's surprising how many avoidable mistakes people make. These tips should be helpful:

- Work on a photocopy of the application form. Copy the information on to the original when you are completely satisfied with what you've written.
- Use black ink and write as neatly as you can. Type it if you can, but the design of forms often makes this impossible. Make sure you eliminate all spelling mistakes. Get someone else to check it.
- Give the information in exactly the way the form asks for it. If, for example, they ask for your most recent experience first, make sure you give it this way around.
- There is always a section where you outline your skills and suitability for the job. Put a lot of time into this and match your abilities to the job's requirements. Keep the job description to hand so you can give the right emphasis.
- Don't leave anything blank. Always fill in the sections where you can give further information. These are a chance to sell your experience. Ignoring them will give the impression that you're not bothered.
- Get your application in early. Missing the deadline means your application will be binned.
- Don't give false information – you will almost certainly be dismissed if found out.
- Keep a copy so you know exactly what you've said.

Applying online

You can apply to some organisations – and the BBC is one of them – via the Internet or by e-mail. There may be an online application form and you may be able to attach or e-mail your CV. Media recruitment agencies, and some companies, may allow you to add your CV and details to a database so they can match your skills to vacancies as they arise.

Some companies allow 'on-spec' applications by e-mail – others do not take kindly to this. Either ring or send a preliminary e-mail to make sure you are not going to annoy anyone by e-mailing your CV.

Put as much time and effort into online applications as written ones – exactly the same level of relevance and accuracy is necessary. Check the format and document type required to ensure your attachments can be opened and read by the recipient.

The Insider guide to performing well at interviews

The vast majority of media employers use interviews as the method for making the final selection. Being called for an interview means your profile on paper fits the requirements for the job. The interview gives the employer a chance to get a more detailed picture of you and to assess whether you would fit in at the company. Always bear in mind that an interview is a two-way process; you are also assessing them and getting a feel for whether this is the kind of place you want to work.

Preparing for the interview

Preparation is the key to a successful interview and can give you an edge over the competition. With adequate preparation you will feel in control of the situation and give a relaxed and confident performance.

- Research the company thoroughly. Read its literature, check out its website, find out about its policies, philosophy, etc.
- Make sure you know every detail about the responsibilities and skill requirements of the job. Find out if any more information is available. Try to get an idea of the sort of person they're looking for.

- The exact nature of the interview can vary – it could be very formal, with a panel of interviewers firing questions, or an informal, one-to-one chat. Try to find out in advance what the format will be, how long it is likely to last, and whether you are required to take any aptitude tests.
- Think about questions you are likely to be asked and plan what you are going to say. Your research into the company and the job should help you with this. Also be prepared for surprises – you may have to think on your feet.
- You will probably need to bring your portfolio of work – employers usually want to see examples of work.
- You will almost certainly be asked if you have any questions. Preparing some intelligent questions shows you are interested and aware.
- Plan your route to the interview location. Make sure you know how long it will take and allow plenty of time. Aim to get there at least 15 minutes early. Arriving late and flustered will mar your performance.

During the interview

- First impressions count. Although some media companies have an informal dress code, you should always dress smartly for an interview. A suit is generally the best policy. You can't lose points for being too smart, but scruffiness could cost you the job. Don't overdo make-up or jewellery.
- Body language is important – sit up straight and make eye contact. Always give a firm handshake (you don't have to break bones). Try to seem keen and enthusiastic. Watch out for any nervous mannerisms and try to smile!
- Nerves can adversely affect your performance. Simple relaxation techniques, such as deep breathing, can be enormously valuable.
- Listen carefully to the questions. Ask for clarification if you haven't understood what the employer wants to find out.

- Keep your answers concise – no waffling – but never just give a yes or no answer. Be positive about yourself without being arrogant or boastful and *don't* criticise your present or former employers.
- If you can't answer a question, be honest about it – but let them know this is something you are keen to learn more about.

After the interview
- If a lot of candidates are being interviewed, it may take some time for the employers to make their selection. Try to find out when they are likely to let you know.
- If you don't get the job, don't get too down about it. There is a huge amount of competition for every media job. Getting an interview means you have the potential, so be persistent. Some companies will give you feedback on why you weren't successful. Get this if you can and make sure you learn from it.
- If you are offered the job, you should be prepared to accept or decline as soon as possible. If you are waiting for the results of other interviews, you can ask for time to think about it. Try to avoid this situation, though, as you may appear half-hearted and this could be held against you.

'I saw the job advertised on an online bulletin board and applied by e-mail. My interview was fairly informal, although I had to do an aptitude test. I found out later that what had impressed them most was my portfolio. It's definitely worth making it look as good as you can.'

Multimedia designer

The Insider guide to performing well at assessment centres

Contrary to the impression the name may give you, an assessment centre is not actually a place. It is a group session run by trained assessors, designed to get a detailed picture of candidates' skills and how they perform in various situations. This is an expensive recruitment technique and, therefore, likely to be used only by larger companies.

The actual format of the session can vary quite a lot but typical activities might include:

- written aptitude tests
- presentations
- group discussions
- group problem-solving tasks and other activities.

There is usually a strong group work focus to assessment centre activities. It is increasingly the case that people employed in the media work in teams on projects, so it is essential that potential employees co-operate well with others and contribute effectively to the group.

- Get involved in all the activities and take them seriously even if you can't immediately see their relevance.
- Make a positive contribution but don't be domineering. Assessors will also be looking for your ability to listen and to encourage and motivate others. Don't try to put others down, even if they are in competition with you for the same job – this will count against you.
- Listen to instructions carefully and make sure you understand what is required. Take time to plan the best way of approaching the task. Be aware of any time limitations.
- Be on your best behaviour all the time you are there. You will probably still be assessed during lunch, coffee breaks or evening meals.
- Remember, it's not just about completing the tasks well – how you interact with others is just as important.

The Insider guide to making presentations

All areas of the media are concerned with effective communication. You may be asked to make a presentation as part of the recruitment process or during an assessment centre.

- Good preparation is the secret of an effective presentation. Research your topic carefully and make sure you understand it fully. If you have a choice of topic, choose something you have a genuine interest in and knowledge of. Your enthusiasm will enliven the talk. Organise the information into clear points, and put it in a logical order. Your presentation should have a clear structure.
- Never read from a script because this will make your presentation very dull and stilted. Write important points out on cards as a memory prompt.
- Use visual aids, such as overheads, to make your points clearer and add visual interest. They also serve as a prompt for you. Keep them fairly simple – no screeds of text, just key points. Use different colours for variety and clarity.
- Make sure you know what equipment will be available and that you are familiar with it. If you can, set up the room in advance. Make sure everyone can see both you and your visual aids.
- Body language is important – make eye contact with everyone and act naturally. Don't move about or gesticulate too much, but try not to look like a shop window mannequin.
- Speak clearly and deliberately – don't rush. Use language that everyone will understand, and avoid jargon. If you need to use technical terms, explain them clearly. Don't be excessively serious, but avoid flippancy. Personal stories can be good if they are relevant, but avoid jokes.
- Practise delivering your talk, preferably in front of people you know. Make sure it fits into the time allowed.

The structure of any presentation should always be basically the same:

- outline what you are going to talk about
- deliver your points in a logical progression
- summarise what you have said
- invite questions.

Pre-interview tests

There are a variety of tests you may encounter during the recruitment process. These may be devised by an employer to see if you have particular skills they need, such as editing or proofreading, or standardised formal assessments that test particular areas in a scientific way. Employers using formal tests may combine a selection of tests to assess different areas of your potential.

There are two main types of test you are likely to encounter.

Aptitude tests

These include a whole variety of test types. They can cover a range of skills, depending on the job in question. If applying for a job that involves computer skills, such as programming, you may be required to do tests that involve mental arithmetic. If the job is journalistic, you may be asked to write a piece in a particular style. Formal aptitude tests commonly encountered include:

- numerical aptitude – mental arithmetic and working with numbers
- verbal aptitude – using and understanding words
- reasoning – applying logic to solve problems
- abstract reasoning – applying logic to abstract tasks
- spatial awareness – understanding and manipulation of shapes
- diagrammatic – logical tests using diagrams.

Psychometric tests

These are designed to give a picture of your character and motivation. They can be used to judge whether you would be likely to be a good 'fit' in the job and the organisation as a whole. Questions may revolve around what you would do in particular situations. There is often no right or wrong answer to these questions.

There are psychometric tests designed to examine a number of areas, such as:

- sociability
- leadership and management potential
- working styles
- career aspirations
- values and attitudes
- teamworking.

Test guidelines

- Tests may be time limited so plan your time carefully. Work out how long you can spend on each question. Bear in mind that questions may get harder towards the end.
- Read the instructions carefully and make sure you follow them.
- Negative marking may apply, which means you lose marks for a wrong answer. If this is the case, avoid guessing if you're not sure of the answer.
- It is usually wise to give honest answers in psychometric tests as you can't always guess the desired response. Generally, you either are or are not the kind of person they're looking for and getting a job under false pretences is not a recipe for career success.
- You can practise some types of aptitude test, and it is certainly an advantage to be familiar with each type of activity. Tests are available through your careers office and on many careers sites on the Internet. The following might be useful:

www.kn.pacbell.com/wired/fil/pages/ listpsychomest.html

www.gla.ac.uk/Otherdepts/Careers psycho.html

MYTH BUSTER
You need a media degree

While media degrees can be useful, particularly if you need specific experience, they are certainly not essential. A media degree is not a passport into media work. Any degree shows a level of intellectual capability and application.

TNT

Case Study
Chief features sub-editor

My route into the newspaper industry was perhaps slightly unconventional. During the school holidays I saw an advert for a junior reporter with the local paper. They were looking for someone aged 16–18, but I decided to apply even although I was only 15 at the time. I had a strong interest in news and sport and was a keen reader of papers. To my great surprise, I was called for an interview and subsequently offered the job. Taking the job meant I would be choosing not to go back to school after the holidays – my original intention had been to continue with my education and probably go on to university. I knew it was a bit of a risk as I would find it hard to return to mainstream education if things didn't work out. My mind was made up though.

I started right at the bottom, making tea, doing the births, deaths and marriages, and even delivering newspapers to the local shops. I had a three-year indenture with the paper, similar to an apprenticeship. Organised training was poor – one course I did get to do was taken on my day off – but I got a lot of extremely valuable hands-on experience very early in my career. I learnt a great deal from some of the older experienced hacks.

I did well and became a district reporter at the age of 18. In those days, you were very much a Jack of all trades and I got a lot of experience in sub-editing. I moved to another paper as news sub-editor, moved into features and eventually became deputy chief of the department. Eventually I needed a move up. Fleet Street was the obvious option but I didn't want to live in London. I moved to a well-respected northern regional paper. Two years later I was promoted to chief features sub-editor – a position I have held for 20 years.

Pay and conditions in the newspaper industry don't compare with some areas of commerce, but there is a buzz you won't find anywhere else. It's an exciting environment and I always look forward to going to work. Shift work is involved as the paper is on the go 24 hours a day. Sometimes you have to work longer hours. This is something you accept as an aspect of the job – it's not a regular nine to five.

Nowadays journalism is a graduate profession. Most people going into it have a degree and a postgraduate qualification in journalism. It's probably harder to get into newspapers now – there are more opportunities in magazines and trade and business journals. You will give yourself an advantage by getting involved in papers as much as you can, for instance working on a student paper or getting work experience at a local paper. This shows you have initiative and motivation.

Newspapers usually offer pretty good training on the job, but to get ahead in your career you will probably have to move around a few different papers. This often means being prepared to move to another area. Working for the nationals generally means you have to live in London.

GETTING ON

Promotion and progression opportunities depend on a number of factors, including your:

- qualifications
- aptitude
- skills and experience
- personality and 'fit'
- desire to learn new skills
- level of determination.

There are also other factors:

- degree of specialisation – there may not be an obvious promotion route from some jobs
- size of company – in smaller companies it can be more difficult to get on
- geographical location – there are more opportunities in certain areas, notably the south-east.

Career paths

It is common for people to advance to the point where the next step would be into management. This can create a dilemma for people in creative or very practical roles who do not want to lose the hands-on element which attracted them to the industry in the first place, and be increasingly concerned with budgets, planning and staff management.

Sideways moves are fairly common. People often shift to a job with a slightly different emphasis, or become more and more specialised in a certain aspect of their work. Some people will find a role they really enjoy and stick with that for the rest of their working career.

Staying with one organisation can be a problem if you want to progress. You may have to change companies in order to develop your career prospects. That being said, there is also a lot to be said for having some stability. If you rush from job to job, some employers will consider you a risk. A company that is going to invest in recruiting and training you wants to know that you will stay with them for a reasonable length of time.

Crossing the media divide

Moving from one area of the media to another is one way to progress. You could move from newspapers into radio, from radio into TV or from TV into multimedia. The ease with which you can do this depends on the blend of skills you have and your determination to get where you want to be.

Geographical location is a definite factor, especially in moving from radio to TV. If you work in an area that doesn't have much in the way of TV production units, you will find it hard to get the experience you need to make the crossover. In some areas, the TV and radio units of, say, the BBC will be located in close proximity – perhaps even in the same building. In this case, it is likely the two will work closely together. You would find more opportunity to get TV experience and would hear what jobs were coming up on the grapevine.

Skills and training

The importance of updating your skills has been a recurring theme throughout this book, but this point cannot be overstated. This is the only way to survive in the media industries. If you really want to make progress, you will also have to learn new skills. Many people get in on the bottom rung of the ladder, perhaps as an assistant or a runner. These are usually poorly paid jobs that they do not want to stay in for long.

The way to move on is to acquire new skills. You may have to be resourceful and self-motivated in order to get these skills, perhaps by persuading someone more senior to let you assist them in order to learn. The only way is to take the bull by the horns – if you know you want to work as an editor or camera operator, you must start to get the experience however you can.

Larger organisations often have better possibilities for training and promotion. BBC staff, for example, have access to excellent structured training and are encouraged to develop new skills. The prospects for promotion and for gaining experience in new areas are very good. Even so, you may still find you need to be resourceful and perhaps do some extra work helping out on other people's projects in order to gain new skills.

Freelances are obviously responsible for their own skills development and must keep up with market needs. This can be problematic in terms of time and money – time spent familiarising yourself with new software, for example, could also be valuable working time. Any courses and qualifications you take will be at your own expense, and could be costly.

Industry qualifications

Qualifications such as NVQs are becoming more widely available for many specific aspects of media work – these include camera work and video editing. These qualifications have not been regarded too seriously in the past but are becoming more widespread in the media. It is likely they will become essential requirements for both media professionals in permanent and freelance employment.

Going freelance

Freelance work is very much a growth area and can provide opportunities for more varied and interesting work. Going freelance can be a good move for people who find themselves in a position where promotion is unlikely. It can, of course, be a risky venture and should not be undertaken lightly. It is important to have good contacts established before you start. Even if you have, things could still be a bit unstable financially for a while. Make sure you are prepared for this and have enough money put by to cover the mortgage payments, bills, etc., at least for the first few months.

Freelancing is covered in more detail in Part Two of this book.

'My background in journalism was what got me into presenting. It gave me the right experience and a certain amount of credibility – I was able to get into TV and radio without having to spend years as a runner or assistant.'

Radio and TV presenter/producer

Case Study
World news co-ordinator for
an online news service

I studied languages and started out as a linguist for radio news with a leading broadcaster. I was very interested in foreign affairs and became increasingly involved in news writing and production in the newsroom.

I became interested in the whole area of the Internet and the new possibilities it could offer. I applied for a job shortly after the Internet service started up. Following a number of tests, involving writing stories at speed, editing and translating, and an interview with a panel, I was appointed and began work about three months into the service's existence.

This is a very exciting area to be working in because it is so new. We are at the pioneering stage – what we are doing hasn't been done before, so we are constantly developing and refining the way we approach things. There are no established precedents. We have the opportunity for a lot of input into the development and direction of the service. Things are changing fast and emerging technology is increasing the scope for what we are able to achieve. Working for a major broadcaster means you have a lot of resources at your disposal. Bringing these to bear on a new medium opens up new and exciting possibilities for the future of news coverage.

My job involves co-ordinating the team, planning coverage of events and developing long-term projects. We seek to make the coverage as good as it can be. Some stories are researched and written from scratch by us. Others come from our journalistic colleagues or news agencies and are adapted to fit the specific requirements of the website. I listen to the world news before coming to work, read the papers on the way in and keep myself updated during the day. The actual structure of a working day varies according to what is happening in the world at that time. I usually attend an editorial meeting to plan the day's priorities. I may spend time writing or rewriting stories, chasing up commission pieces or collating background information for upcoming projects.

Working as a team is essential – there isn't the same hierarchical management structure you find in some areas. A strong interest in news is essential, as is the ability to write clear and concise copy. Accuracy, speed and an eye for detail are very important. Stamina definitely helps as the work can be quite pressurised. The continuous nature of news coverage means there are ongoing deadlines to meet. A good track record in journalism is required for people wanting to work on the news side of things, as well as some knowledge of the technology and an aptitude to learn. The more skills you have the better – people need to be able to write, produce and edit stories, find pictures then crop and adapt them, and edit audio. There are a lot of different strands to the work.

Most of the people working here are quite young – typically in their 20s and early 30s. I am one of the oldest at 38.

I am happy where I am at the moment – it's a new and challenging field. In the future I might think about moving into another Internet area, perhaps a smaller company where I could have more overall control. A big organisation has a lot of advantages but you do have to adapt and fit in with its way of working.

GETTING OUT

The media industries tend to be the ones everybody wants to get into rather than out of. A passion for working in the industry is a key feature of people working in various aspects of the media. The vast majority of people love the work and want to continue doing it in some form. And because the media industry is so vast and covers so many very different areas of work, you can actually effect a radical career change without leaving the media altogether.

So what are your options if you do decide you want to embark on a career in a completely different industry? Well, that depends very much on the area you work in and your experience. However, people working in most areas of the media tend to acquire skills such as good communication, teamworking, time management and working to deadlines. These are very transferable and highly sought after in any industry. These days, the media and communications are a vital aspect of many areas of business and industry. People with media experience are in increasing demand.

The convergence of the media, ICT and telecommunications industries is creating more possibilities for people wanting to change direction. People with a high level of computer skills acquired in media could move wholeheartedly into computing and ICT. Those who have worked extensively in Internet and interactive media related areas could move into the telecommunications sector.

An area open to people with experience in aspects of broadcasting is the theatre. If you have experience in any aspect of sound, lighting, set construction, design, direction, etc., you could move into this work. People such as radio or TV studio managers can transfer their skills to managing productions or entire theatres.

Advertising and PR are two of the most common areas for people with media experience to move into. Press officers commonly have a background in journalism or broadcasting. These areas have a need for people with a creative background, for 'ideas people' capable of original thought and able to meet deadlines. People with a journalistic background can make the transition into advertising copywriting.

We have seen that freelance work is common to all the media industries. Being self employed in the media will give you skills that could be transferred to many areas of business and finance. Starting your own small business in a completely different area of work could also be a strong possibility – you would be able to demonstrate business sense that can help in convincing banks and venture capitalists of the viability of your scheme.

Case Study
Freelance features writer

I studied English at university and followed this up with a postgraduate qualification in journalism. My first experience was writing for the university's student paper. This was actually pretty useful – it certainly helps you to get a basic grounding.

After my studies, I travelled around Australia for a year and managed to get work with a number of local newspapers along the way – this was my first taste of real journalism and I enjoyed it immensely. I applied for a number of jobs when I got back to the UK and was taken on by a trade magazine. My experience gained working abroad was probably the crucial factor in getting me the job.

I stayed with the magazine for two and a half years and gained some valuable experience in that time. However, I found working in the trade press increasingly dull, so I decided to get out. Going freelance seemed like the right move for me – I wanted more independence and more variety in my work. Getting established wasn't actually that hard – I had some good contacts already and got a good response from editors I contacted with feature ideas.

I contribute regular features to national papers including The Sunday Times and the Daily Mail, as well as writing for an online business service and a variety of magazines. I also teach writing for magazines at a London college.

You need to be very self-motivated to be successful as a freelance. At the end of the day, there's just you – you don't have anyone to tell you what to do or help you plan your career. You need to be flexible and able to adapt to different styles of writing. Also, you must not be too precious about your work. If an editor pulls your article apart you must accept this with good grace.

The media are very stimulating industries to work in. New developments are happening fast and there are exciting opportunities for people willing to take up the challenge. You will have realised that there is a lot of competition for jobs, but you should not let this put you off. If you are determined to do well and prepared to use your initiative to learn the skills you need, there is no reason why you should not be successful.

This book is intended to give you a taster of the world of media and to provide some pointers on how to get your media career off the ground. You will need to do some further research of your own. On the following pages are the details of some publications and organisations that may be helpful. Good luck!

JARGON BUSTER

The media industries are not without their technical jargon. If you are planning a career in media it is helpful to have some knowledge of the terminology you are likely to come across. This is not a comprehensive glossary but it will give you an understanding of some widely used terms.

3D modelling
Computer graphics software capable of creating 3D objects, built up around an outline frame, that can be rotated in space. Objects can be given textures and lit in various ways.

Acceleration editing
Creating the appearance of time being expanded or condensed through editing – e.g. when a scene that takes place in just a few minutes is made to last much longer than that for dramatic effect.

Access channels
Cable TV channels used for local community programming.

Action cutting
An editing technique that cuts from one shot to another to make it look as though numerous cameras are being used.

Actuality
Live footage of an out-of-studio event.

Ambient sound
The prevailing background sound at a location.

Amplitude modulation (AM)
Broadcasting technique that modifies the height of the carrier wave. Sound quality is not as good as FM.

Analogue signal
A signal with a continuous pattern that has a precise relationship to the original information source.

Analogue to digital conversion (ADC)
The conversion of an analogue signal to digital data.

Audience profile
The breakdown of a programme's audience by demographic categories.

Bandwidth
The amount of information that can be sent through a channel or connection, usually measured in bits per second.

Bit
Short for binary digit – a single digit number in binary code, i.e. a one or a zero. The smallest unit of computerised data.

Boom
A long adjustable pole from which a TV studio microphone is suspended.

Bps
Bits per second – a measurement of the speed of data transfer.

Broadsheet
A newspaper approximately 15 inches wide and 22 inches in height. This term normally refers to 'serious' papers such as *The Times*, *The Guardian*, etc. See also *tabloid*.

CAD
Computer-Aided Design. Software systems for designing in 3D.

Clapperboard
Hinged board used at the start of a take when shooting with film. The clapperboard provides a reference for synchronising sound and vision – the sound of the clap is aligned with the visual action of it being made.

Controlled circulation
Magazines, papers and other publications restricted to a particular target audience. Includes trade magazines.

Copy
The text for a printed publication.

Coverage area
The area within which a TV or radio station can be received. Also refers to the area served by a regional newspaper.

Cross-fade
A TV editing technique for moving from one shot to another. The previous shot is faded out and the next is simultaneously faded in. Also referred to as dissolve or mix.

Cyberspace
A term coined by author William Gibson in his novel *Neuromancer*. Refers to the 'virtual' realm of computer networks and systems.

DAB
Digital Audio Broadcasting (digital radio).

DAT
Digital Audio Tape. Tape on which digital sound can be recorded.

Desktop publishing (DTP)
Computer software used for design, page layout and graphics.

Digital broadcasting
System of TV and radio broadcasting that transmits information as a numerical binary code.

Dissolve
See *cross-fade.*

Docusoap
A fly-on-the-wall style of documentary making that invites viewers to follow the lives of ordinary people.

Dolly
A camera mounting similar to a crane arm that allows movement in all directions.

Domain name
The address locating a website on the Internet. Consists of a name and a suffix separated by dots, e.g. **indsoc.co.uk**

Dubbing
The transfer of a magnetic audio or visual signal from one tape to another.

Editing
The process of cutting, modifying and sequencing audio and/ or visual footage for broadcast. Also the selection and adaptation of text for publication.

ENG
Electronic News Gathering. Reports are filmed with an electronic camera. Footage may be transmitted back directly to the studio or broadcast live.

Feature
An in-depth article, often with a 'lifestyle' rather than direct news slant, usually illustrated with photos.

Format
The style or genre of a TV or radio show, e.g. sitcom, docusoap, etc.

Four colour
Printing technique that reproduces full colour using a combination of black, blue, yellow and red.

Frame
An individual unit picture on a piece of film footage or animation. The lines scanned on a video recording.

Frequency modulation (FM)
Radio broadcasting technique which alters the number of waves per second. Allows better sound quality than AM.

Gaffer
The chief electrician in a TV studio.

Genre
A style of film or TV programme making, e.g. film noir, period drama, etc.

GIF
Graphic Interchange Format. A format for graphics files. Less suitable for photographic images than *JPEG* but uses less memory.

Giraffe
An extending microphone boom mounted on a wheeled tripod base.

Graphics
Images, usually created on computer.

Hack
A reporter. Usually refers to the old-style reporter dressed in shabby overcoat and trilby.

HTML
HyperText Markup Language. Internet programming language used to create web page documents.

HTTP
HyperText Transfer Protocol. The protocol for transferring hypertext files across the Internet.

Hypertext
Text containing links to other documents or locations on the web.

Idiot board
A board with cues for a TV presenter.

ILR
Independent Local Radio. Umbrella term for commercial radio stations.

ISDN
Integrated Services Digital Network. System for sending digital data via phone lines.

ITC
Independent Television Commission. Set up following the 1991 Broadcasting Act, the ITC is the regulating body for commercial TV in the UK.

JPEG
Joint Photographic Expert Group. A format for graphics files. Allows for high definition photographic images. See also *GIF*.

Limbo
TV studio technique that uses plain backgrounds to give a feeling of expansive space.

Location
A TV or radio broadcast or recording site away from the studio.

Mix
See *cross-fade*.

Montage
A composite graphic or photographic image. Also the process of selecting and piecing together material for a film.

Network
A group of linked radio or TV stations that broadcast simultaneously. Also refers to a number of linked computers.

NRS
National Readership Survey. Conducted annually to estimate the readership of more than 200 consumer publications.

Out take
A scene that is edited out of the final production.

Pan
A horizontal camera sweep. See also *tilt*.

Pilot
A trial episode of a planned TV series used to forecast the likely popularity level of the series.

Prime time
The peak TV viewing hours, approximately from 8pm to 11pm.

Proof
A copy of a publication or other printed matter used for checking purposes.

Proofreading
Checking copy for mistakes.

Public service broadcasting (PSB)
System under which specified obligations to the viewer are legally protected.

RA
Radio Authority. Regulating body for UK commercial radio.

RAJAR
Radio Joint Audience Research. Company set up to manage the UK's radio audience measurement system.

Repackaging
Reworking archive material or previously used footage to create a new programme.

RGB
Red, green and blue. The system of coloured phosphors used in cathode ray tube TVs and computer monitors.

Rifle mic
Long-range microphone mounted on a long tube. A rifle mic is very directional and can separate a specific sound from the background sound.

Rushes
Raw, unedited TV or film footage. So called because there would be a rush to get a print for viewing so the director could make any reshooting decisions.

Stills
Non-moving pictures. Can refer to either photographs or individual frames from film or video footage.

Storyboard
A rough outline structure of a TV programme showing possible scenes and shots, usually drawn in the form of a cartoon strip.

Tabloid
A smaller size newspaper, usually 14 inches high, often with a populist or sensationalist slant. Examples include *The Sun* and the *News of the World*.

Talking heads
Head-and-shoulder close-up shots of people talking to camera. Commonly used in interviews.

Tilt
A vertical movement of the camera. See also *pan*.

UHF
Ultra High Frequency. A frequency used for conventional TV broadcasting.

VHF
Very High Frequency. Used for some radio broadcasting and until the mid 1980s for black and white 405 line TV broadcasting.

Voice-over
A narrative recorded over a piece of footage.

Vox pop
The views of the public, obtained in on-the-street interviews.

VTR
Video Tape Recorder.

Watershed
The time before which programmes with content unsuitable for children may not be broadcast. The UK has a 9pm watershed.

Wild track
Sound, usually on location, which is recorded separately and edited in later.

WANT TO FIND OUT MORE?

On the following pages you will find some websites, publications and organisations to help you get started on your career research.

Useful websites

Careers

University of Sussex
www.sussex.ac.uk/Units/CDU/cimedi.html

Milkround Online
www.milkround.com/s1/firms/index.html

Prospects
www.prospects.csu.ac.uk

Careerworld
www.careerworld.net

Media links

The Press Association
www.pa.press.net/news/media/main.html

Media UK Directory
www.mediauk.com/directory

Media Contacts
www.l-m-c.org.uk/resources/contacts.html

Useful organisations

BBC Recruitment Services
PO Box 7000
London W12 8GJ
020 7580 4468
www.bbc.co.uk

British Film Institute (BFI)
21 Stephen Street
London WIP 2LN
020 7255 1444
www.bfi.org.uk

Broadcasting, Entertainment, Cinematography and Theatre
Union (BECTU)
111 Wardour Street
London
W1V 4AY
020 7437 8506
www.bectu.org.uk
The major union for broadcasting, film and theatre
professionals.

Commercial Radio Companies Association (CRCA)
77 Shaftesbury Avenue
London W1V 7AD
020 7306 2603
www.crca.co.uk

Community Media Association
15 Paternoster Row
Sheffield S1 2BX
0114 279 5219
www.commedia.org.uk

National Council for the Training of Journalists (NCTJ)
Latton Bush Centre
Southern Way
Harlow
Essex CM18 7BL
01279 430009
www.nctj.com/

National Union of Journalists (NUJ)
Acorn House
314–320 Grays Inn Road
London WC1X 8DP
020 7278 7916
www.nuj.org.uk
The major union for journalists and writers.

The Radio Academy
5 Market Place
London W1N 7AH
020 7255 2010
www.radioacademy.org
Professional body for those working in, or with an interest in, radio.

Skillset
2nd Floor
103 Dean Street
London W1V 5RA
020 7534 5300
www.skillset.org
National training organisation for broadcast, film, video and multimedia.

WANT TO READ ALL ABOUT IT?

Newspapers and magazines

Ariel
In-house magazine of the BBC – available by subscription from the BBC.

Broadcast
Weekly magazine for the broadcasting industry.

The Guardian
Media section on Mondays.

New Media Age
Magazine for the electronic media industry.

Press Gazette
Weekly paper for journalists – covers print and broadcasting.

Books

The Guardian Media Guide, Fourth Estate for *The Guardian*. Published annually. Available from major bookshops and from *The Guardian*.

Skillset Careers Handbook, Skillset.
Available from Skillset, see page 117.

Writers' and Artists' Yearbook, A&C Black.
Published annually. Available widely from bookshops and libraries.

The Insider Career Guides

Advertising, Marketing and PR
Karen Holmes
ISBN 1 85835 872 8

Banking and the City
Karen Holmes
ISBN 1 85835 583 4

Broadcasting and the Media
Paul Redstone
ISBN 1 85835 867 1

The Environment
Melanie Allen
ISBN 1 85835 588 5

Information and Communications Technology
Jacquetta Megarry
ISBN 1 85835 593 1

Retailing
Liz Edwards
ISBN 1 85835 578 8

Sport
Robin Hardwick
ISBN 1 85835 573 7

Travel and Tourism
Karen France
ISBN 1 85835 598 2

These and other Industrial Society titles are available from all good bookshops or direct from The Industrial Society on telephone 0870 400 1000 (p&p charges apply).